Invisible Journeys
Sound
Caroline Grimshaw
TEXT EDITOR IQBAL HUSSAIN
SCIENCE CONSULTANT JOHN STRINGER
World Book
in association with
TWOCAN

Sound

CREATIVE AND EDITORIAL DIRECTOR
CONCEPT/FORMAT/DESIGN/TEXT
CAROLINE GRIMSHAW

TEXT EDITOR IQBAL HUSSAIN
SCIENCE CONSULTANT JOHN STRINGER
ILLUSTRATIONS
NICK DUFFY ✱ SPIKE GERRELL
CAROLINE GRIMSHAW
THANKS TO
TIM SANPHER COMPUTER IMAGERY
LAURA CARTWRIGHT PICTURE RESEARCH
MELISSA TUCKER U.S. EDITOR, WORLD BOOK PUBLISHING

TITLES IN THIS SERIES
✱ SUN
✱ COMMUNICATION
✱ SOUND
✱ ENERGY

PUBLISHED IN THE UNITED STATES BY
WORLD BOOK, INC., 525 W. MONROE, CHICAGO, IL 60661
IN ASSOCIATION WITH TWO-CAN PUBLISHING LTD.

LIBRARY OF CONGRESS CATALOGING-IN-PUBLICATION DATA
GRIMSHAW, CAROLINE
SOUND / CAROLINE GRIMSHAW; [ILLUSTRATIONS NICK DUFFY, SPIKE GERRELL, CAROLINE GRIMSHAW].
P. CM. -- (INVISIBLE JOURNEYS)
SUMMARY: QUESTIONS AND ANSWERS AND ACTIVITIES EXPLORE THE DEFINITION, CAUSE, EFFECTS, AND USES OF SOUND.
ISBN 0-7166-3006-0 (HARDCOVER). -- ISBN 0-7166-3007-9 (SOFTCOVER)
1. SOUND--MISCELLANEA--JUVENILE LITERATURE. [1. SOUND--MISCELLANEA. 2. QUESTIONS AND ANSWERS.] I. DUFFY, NICK, ILL. II. GERRELL, SPIKE, ILL. III. TITLE. IV. SERIES
QC225.5G75 1998
534--dc21 97-51965

HARDBACK 1 2 3 4 5 6 7 8 9 10 01 00 99 98
PAPERBACK 1 2 3 4 5 6 7 8 9 10 01 00 99 98

PRINTED IN SPAIN

I am your Route Scout. I will show you the way. Look out for my two companions on your journey.

Welcome TO Invisible Journeys

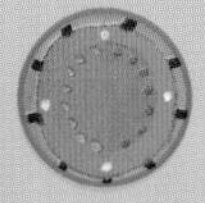

THE *Highway*

Travel along the *Highway* following a sound's journey from its source (the sound itself) to its end (the people).

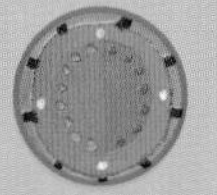

THE Side Roads

On your journey you will be asked to select your own route. Choose a Side Road and follow its route.

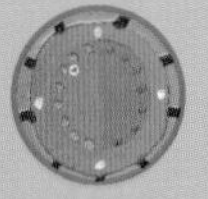

THE Road Stops

The Side Roads lead you to Road Stops, which contain vital information about your trip. These may lead you farther on to the Points of Interest, which are bursting with fascinating facts. Visible Proof Spots will test your knowledge with experiments and puzzles. Detours allow you to leap forward to Road Stops farther along the route. They have a symbol that looks like this. ------→ Deto

Let's examine sound!

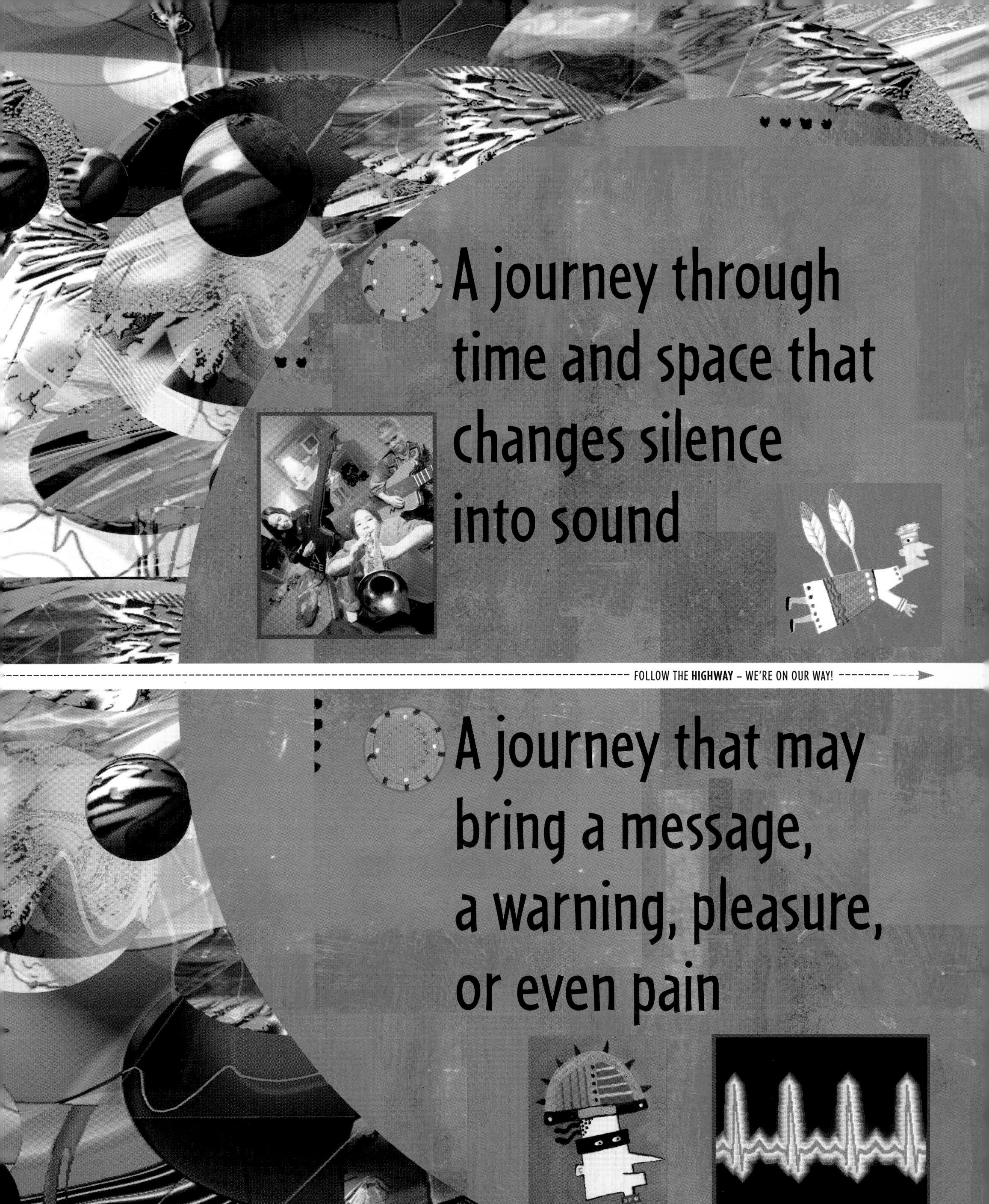

A journey through time and space that changes silence into sound

A journey that may bring a message, a warning, pleasure, or even pain

A whisper, the rustling of leaves, the roar of a jet engine, the boom of a bass drum – all of these are

FOLLOW THE **HIGHWAY**.

sounds.

Our journey begins at the point at which sound is made.

Sounds are all around us. Let's examine what they are and where they come from.

Select YOUR SIDE ROAD

The Sound

1 What is sound? (WHAT ARE SOUND WAVES?) — SIDE ROAD TO ROAD STOP 1

2 How do we describe sound? (HOW DO WE WRITE IT DOWN?) — SIDE ROAD TO ROAD STOP 2

3 How have people studied sound?

4 Can we see sound? (CAN WE FEEL IT?) — SIDE ROAD TO ROAD STOP 4

5 What different ways are there of making sound? — SIDE ROAD TO ROAD STOP 5

6 Why is sound so important to us? — SIDE ROAD TO ROAD STOP 6

Just think!

Not only can we hear sound, we can also feel it – and see it too!

ROAD STOP

1

What is sound?

Sound is anything that can be heard. Every sound is made by something moving rapidly back and forth. These movements are called vibrations and are usually too small to see.

Visible Proof SPOT

Sound is made when an object vibrates. Place a ruler over the edge of a table and twang it. As the ruler vibrates, it produces a whirring sound. When the vibrations stop, so does the sound.

Detour

CAN WE FEEL SOUND VIBRATIONS? LEAP TO **ROAD STOP 4**.

VIBRATIONS AND SOUND

※ As an object vibrates, it causes the air around it to vibrate.

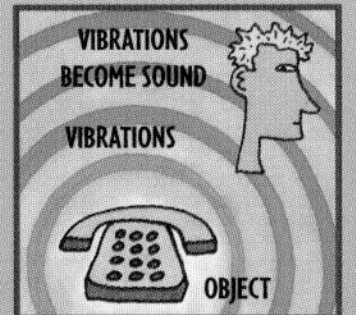

※ When the vibrating air reaches our ears, the brain interprets it as sound.

HOW DOES SOUND TRAVEL? FOLLOW THE PATH TO THE **POINT OF INTEREST**.

Striking a drum with sticks makes it vibrate, producing a thumping sound.

Detour

SOUND TRAVELS THROUGH AIR, BUT IT CAN ALSO MOVE THROUGH SOLIDS AND LIQUIDS. LEAP TO **ROAD STOP 7**.

FOLLOW THE **HIGHWAY**.

POINT of Interest

Sound moves in waves.

What are sound waves?

If you drop a pebble into still water, waves spread out from the point where the pebble hits the surface. Sound travels through the air in a similar series of waves.

1 When a vibrating object moves outward, it squeezes the air molecules (tiny particles) near it. This is called an area of compression.

2 As the object moves inward, air molecules are more spread out in the space left behind. This is called an area of rarefaction.

3 Sound waves are made up of the series of compressions and rarefactions produced by the object, as it continues to move outward and inward.

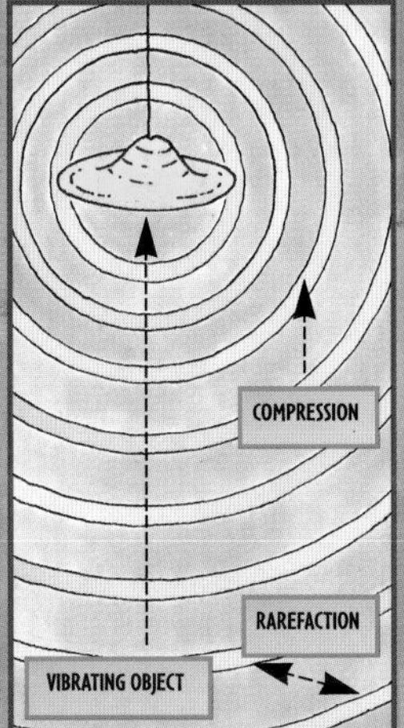

Visible Proof SPOT

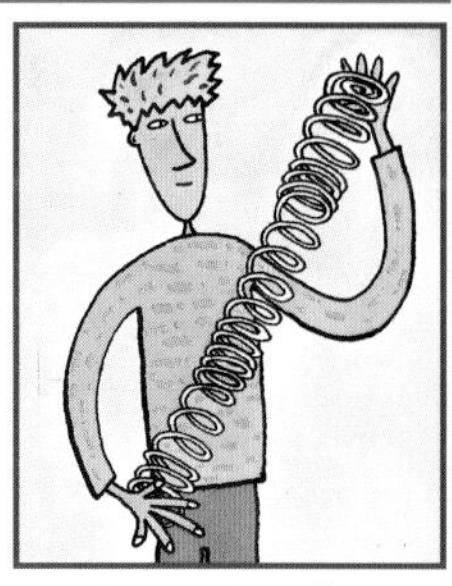

Sound waves move by squeezing and stretching. Hold a spring or a strip of paper folded like an accordion. When you pull one end in and out, it alternately bunches together (making compressions) and stretches out (making rarefactions).

WHAT IS A DECIBEL? **SIDE ROAD** TO ROAD STOP 2

WHO GAVE HIS NAME TO A MEASUREMENT OF SOUND? **SIDE ROAD** TO ROAD STOP 3

HOW CAN WE SEE SOUND WAVES? **SIDE ROAD** TO ROAD STOP 4

WHAT DIFFERENT WAYS ARE THERE OF MAKING SOUNDS? **SIDE ROAD** TO ROAD STOP 5

WHY DO WE NEED SOUND? **SIDE ROAD** TO ROAD STOP 6

ROAD STOP 2

How do we describe sound?

In addition to describing sound as loud or soft, we can examine its frequency, pitch, intensity, and quality.

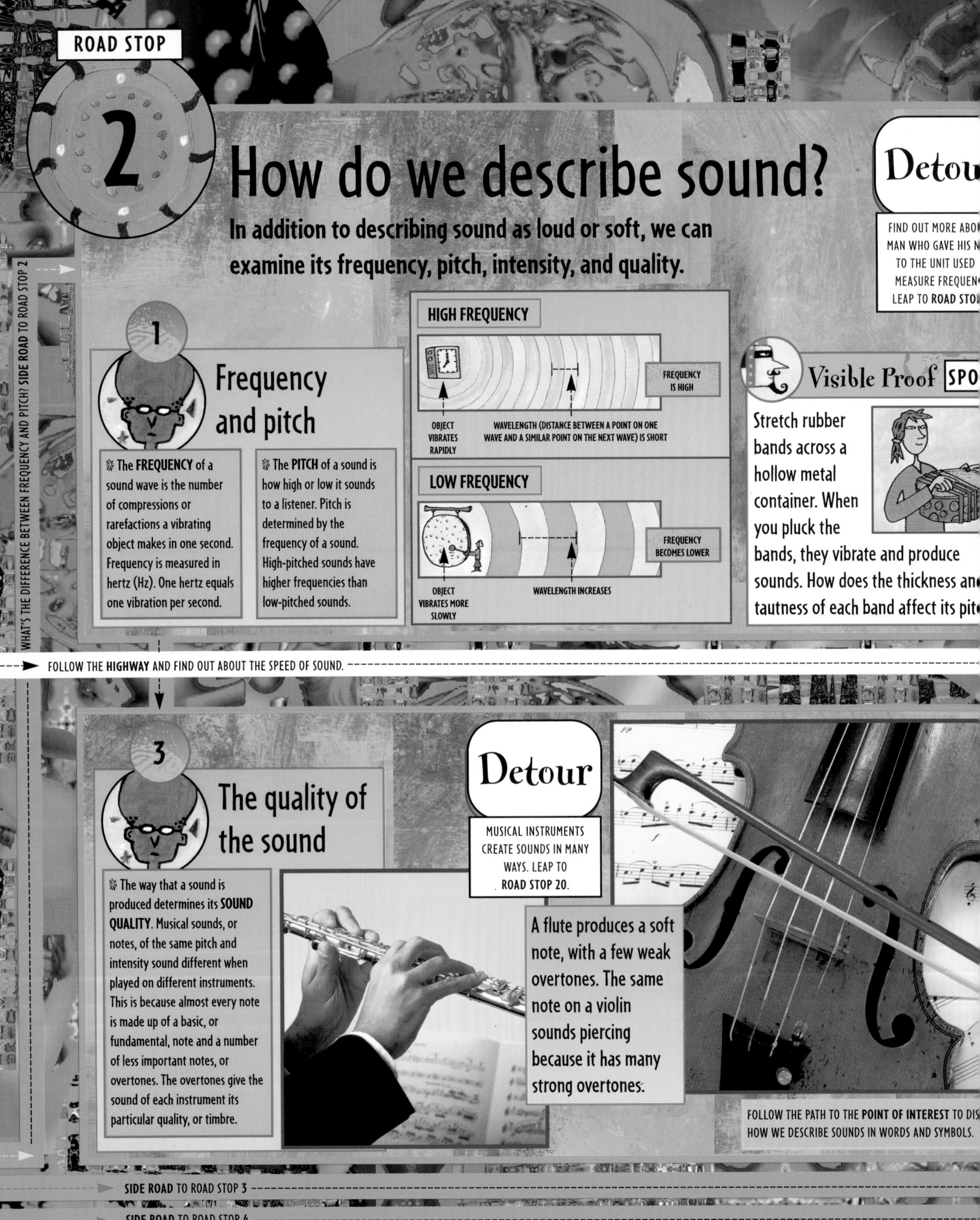

Detou

FIND OUT MORE ABO MAN WHO GAVE HIS N TO THE UNIT USED MEASURE FREQUEN LEAP TO **ROAD STO**

1 Frequency and pitch

The **FREQUENCY** of a sound wave is the number of compressions or rarefactions a vibrating object makes in one second. Frequency is measured in hertz (Hz). One hertz equals one vibration per second.

The **PITCH** of a sound is how high or low it sounds to a listener. Pitch is determined by the frequency of a sound. High-pitched sounds have higher frequencies than low-pitched sounds.

Visible Proof SPO

Stretch rubber bands across a hollow metal container. When you pluck the bands, they vibrate and produce sounds. How does the thickness an tautness of each band affect its pit

WHAT'S THE DIFFERENCE BETWEEN FREQUENCY AND PITCH? **SIDE ROAD** TO ROAD STOP 2

FOLLOW THE **HIGHWAY** AND FIND OUT ABOUT THE SPEED OF SOUND.

3 The quality of the sound

The way that a sound is produced determines its **SOUND QUALITY**. Musical sounds, or notes, of the same pitch and intensity sound different when played on different instruments. This is because almost every note is made up of a basic, or fundamental, note and a number of less important notes, or overtones. The overtones give the sound of each instrument its particular quality, or timbre.

Detour

MUSICAL INSTRUMENTS CREATE SOUNDS IN MANY WAYS. LEAP TO **ROAD STOP 20.**

A flute produces a soft note, with a few weak overtones. The same note on a violin sounds piercing because it has many strong overtones.

FOLLOW THE PATH TO THE **POINT OF INTEREST** TO DIS HOW WE DESCRIBE SOUNDS IN WORDS AND SYMBOLS.

SIDE ROAD TO ROAD STOP 3

SIDE ROAD TO ROAD STOP 4

SIDE ROAD TO ROAD STOP 5

SIDE ROAD TO ROAD STOP 6

2 Intensity and loudness

The sound of falling leaves may measure only 10 decibels.

※ The **INTENSITY** of a sound is the amount of energy carried in the sound waves. The larger the distance a vibrating object moves from its resting position, the more intense the sound.

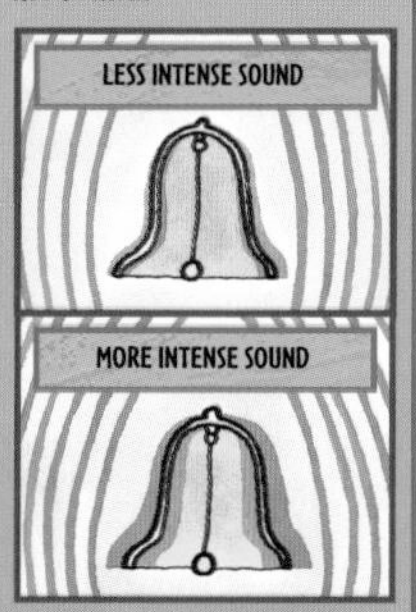

AMPLITUDE = DISTANCE AN OBJECT MOVES AWAY FROM ITS ORIGINAL POSITION AS IT VIBRATES

※ The **LOUDNESS** of a sound is how strong it sounds to someone listening to it. The more intense a sound is, the louder it seems. The greater the distance between the source of the sound and the person hearing it, the softer the sound.

MEASURING SOUND INTENSITY

The intensity of a sound is measured in decibels (dB). Each 10 dB added to a sound multiplies its intensity by 10. So, a 20 dB sound is 10 times as intense as a 10 dB sound, while a 30 dB sound is 100 times (10 x 10) as intense as a 10 dB sound.

EXAMINING INTENSITY

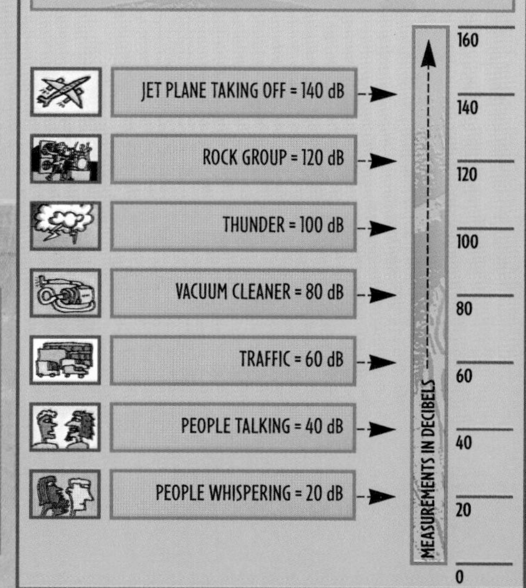

Visible Proof SPOT

Turn on a radio and ask a friend to walk away from you with the radio still playing. Notice how the sound gradually fades.

FOLLOW THE **HIGHWAY**.

POINT of Interest

Sounds can be captured on paper.

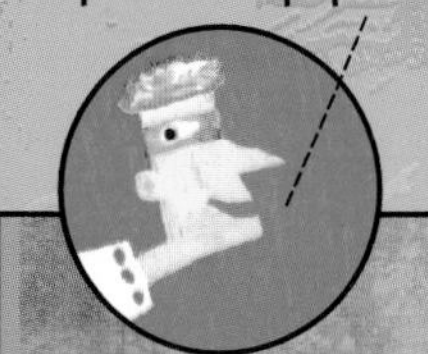

How do we write down sounds?

There are many ways of writing down or describing sounds.

IMITATING SOUNDS

We can use words that copy the sound they are describing. This is called onomatopoeia.

EXAMPLES: "CUCKOO," "BANG," "SPLASH," "HISS."

USING SIMILES

A simile is a way of describing one thing by comparing it to another.

EXAMPLE: "SHE SANG LIKE A NIGHTINGALE."

GIVING INSTRUCTIONS

Composers write down music using a special code, called notation.

※ NOTES ARE WRITTEN ON AND BETWEEN FIVE LINES, CALLED A STAFF OR STAVE. EACH LINE AND SPACE REPRESENTS A DIFFERENT PITCH.

※ THE SHAPE OF A NOTE SHOWS HOW LONG IT IS TO BE PLAYED.

※ WORDS AND SIGNS DESCRIBE HOW THE MUSIC SHOULD BE PLAYED. EXAMPLES:
PIANISSIMO (PP) = VERY SOFTLY
FORTE (F) = LOUDLY
CRESCENDO (<) = GETTING LOUDER.

SOME PEOPLE SPEND THEIR LIVES STUDYING SOUND. **SIDE ROAD** TO ROAD STOP 3
AS WELL AS BEING HEARD, SOUND CAN BE SEEN AND FELT, TOO! **SIDE ROAD** TO ROAD STOP 4
SOUND FROM INSIDE THE BODY! **SIDE ROAD** TO ROAD STOP 5
SOUND CAN WARN US OF TROUBLE AHEAD. **SIDE ROAD** TO ROAD STOP 6

ROAD STOP

3 How have people studied sound?

Scientists and great thinkers, or philosophers, have studied sound since ancient times. Their discoveries have changed people's understanding of how sound is produced and heard.

WHO MADE IMPORTANT DISCOVERIES ABOUT SOUND? SIDE ROAD TO ROAD STOP 3

1

PYTHAGORAS (580? B.C. - ?B.C.)

Pythagoras was a Greek philosopher and mathematician. He carried out experiments to find out how the length of a stretched string affected the sound it made when it vibrated.

2

ARISTOTLE (384-322 B.C.)

This Greek philosopher suggested that sound is carried to our ears by the movement of air.

3

LEONARDO DA VINCI (1452-1519)

This Italian painter and scientist helped to develop the theory that sound travels in waves.

4

GALILEO GALILEI (1564-16

This Italian astronomer and scientist discovered that the frequency of sound waves determines their pitch.

FOLLOW THE **HIGHWAY**.

ROAD STOP

4 Can we see sound?

Machines can create pictures of sound waves, even though they are invisible in the air. We can also see the effects of sound waves.

THE OSCILLOSCOPE

An oscilloscope is a machine that shows sound waves as electrical signals. These signals appear on a screen as wavy lines that change as the sound itself changes.

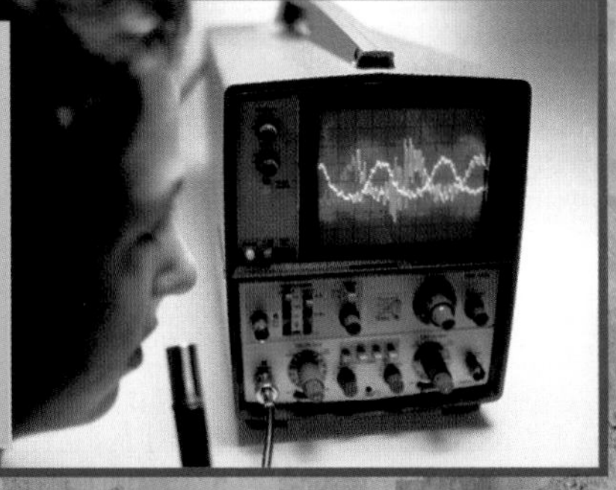

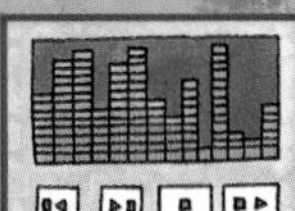

A stereo system often has a screen that displays the changing sound levels produced by music or speech.

Visible Proof SPOT

When sound waves hit an object, they make it vibrate. Stretch a piece of plast across a bowl and secure it with a rubb band. Sprinkle some salt on the plastic. Now make a loud sound by holding a metal pan close to the bowl and bangi it. The sound waves from the lid strike the plastic and make it vibrate. This causes the salt crystals to jump.

CAN WE FEEL SOUND VIBRATIONS? FO THE PATH TO THE **POINT OF INTERES**

SIDE ROAD TO ROAD STOP 3
SIDE ROAD TO ROAD STOP 4
SIDE ROAD TO ROAD STOP 5
SIDE ROAD TO ROAD STOP 6

Visible Proof SPOT

Press a glass to a closed door, then place your ear to the bottom of the glass. You should hear sounds inside the room much louder than by just listening with your ears. Sound waves from the room are carried directly to your ear through the door and the glass.

ACOUSTICS

Acoustics is the science of sound – how it is created, transmitted, and received.

MARIN MERSENNE (1588–1648)

This French monk and mathematician was the first to estimate the speed of sound. He asked a fellow monk to fire a gun a known distance away, then calculated how long it took for him to hear the bang after seeing the flash of the gun.

6

ROBERT BOYLE (1627–1691)

This Irish scientist showed that sound waves need some kind of matter, or medium, to travel through. He pumped out the air from a jar containing a ticking watch. When the air was completely removed, the ticking could no longer be heard.

Detour

THERE IS NO AIR IN SPACE, SO HOW DO ASTRONAUTS TALK TO EACH OTHER? DETOUR TO **ROAD STOP 7**.

7

HEINRICH HERTZ (1857–1894)

This German scientist discovered radio waves, which paved the way for the invention of radio. The unit of frequency used for all waves and vibrations is named after him.

FOLLOW THE **HIGHWAY** TO FIND OUT HOW THE SPEED OF SOUND DEPENDS ON THE MEDIUM THROUGH WHICH IT TRAVELS.

POINT of Interest

Feel the ground move!

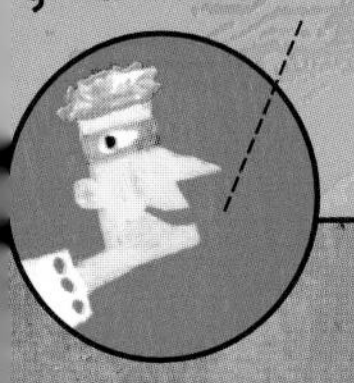

Can we feel sound?

Some sound waves are so loud and intense that they are felt as well as heard.

Heavy traffic, such as large trucks and high-speed trains, can produce powerful sound waves. Traffic generates between 60 and 90 dB of noise. This may penetrate the walls and windows of nearby buildings and cause the furniture inside to vibrate!

Detour

SOME SOUNDS CAN BE DANGEROUS. DETOUR TO **ROAD STOP 18**.

HOW DOES A BEE BUZZ? **SIDE ROAD** TO ROAD STOP 5

SOUND HELPS US TO EXPERIENCE THE WORLD. **SIDE ROAD** TO ROAD STOP 6

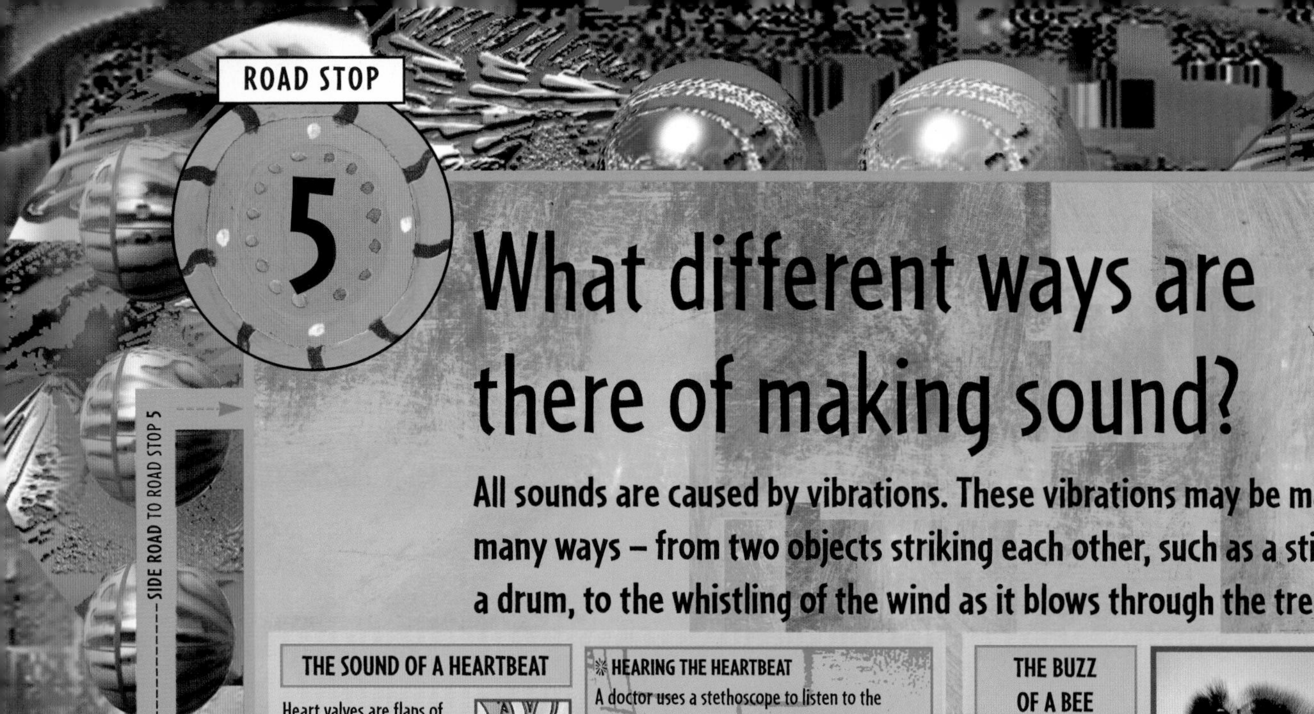

ROAD STOP

5

What different ways are there of making sound?

Detou

FIND OUT HOW PEOP
TURN SOUND INTO SPE
DETOUR TO
ROAD STOP 21.

All sounds are caused by vibrations. These vibrations may be made in many ways – from two objects striking each other, such as a stick banging a drum, to the whistling of the wind as it blows through the trees.

THE SOUND OF A HEARTBEAT

Heart valves are flaps of tissue that open and shut to control the flow of blood through the heart. The sound of a heartbeat is the sound of the valves closing as blood flows through the heart.

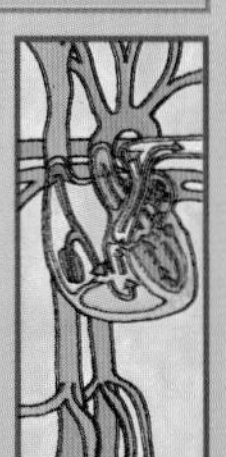

HEARING THE HEARTBEAT

A doctor uses a stethoscope to listen to the soft sounds of a person's heartbeat. A stethoscope is a rubber tube with a small, flat funnel at one end and a pair of earpieces at the other.

THE BUZZ OF A BEE

The buzzing sound of bees and many other flying insects is made by the vibrations of their wings beating rapidly against the air.

SIDE ROAD TO ROAD STOP 5

FOLLOW THE **HIGHWAY** AND FIND OUT HOW SOUND TRAVELS.

ROAD STOP

6

Why is sound so important to us?

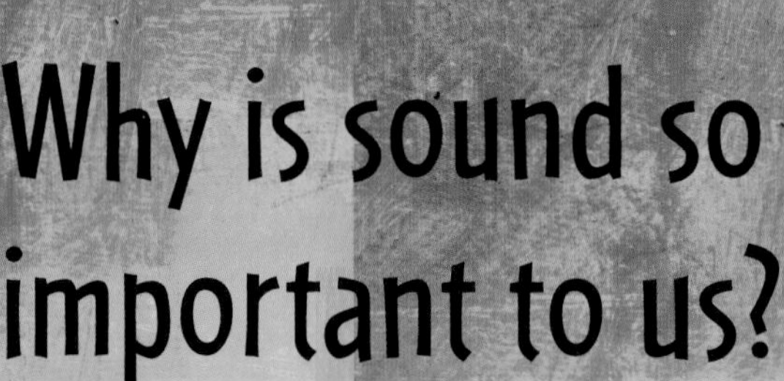

Detour

TO DISCOVER HOW WE HEAR SOUND, DETOUR TO ROAD STOP 10.

People use sound to communicate with each other. Some sounds act as warning devices, and others help to catch someone's attention. Sound can be stimulating or relaxing.

Visible Proof SP

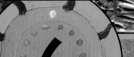

Language is our most common form of communication. Without speaking, try to tell a friend about a book you have read. How easy is it to relay t information using just gestures?

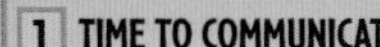

1 TIME TO COMMUNICATE

- Early people probably communicated with one another by making basic sounds such as grunts, barks, and hoots.
- Today, almost six billion people live on the planet. There are about 6,000 different languages in the world and thousands more dialects, which are local variations of languages.

2 WATCH OUT!

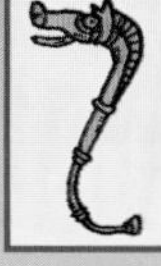

- The ancient Celts used sound to help them in their wars against the Romans. In the heat of battle, Celtic warriors would blow large, trumpetlike instruments, called carnyxes. These produced a tremendous, screaming din that terrified the Roman soldiers!

3 LISTEN UP!

- Some machines use devices such as bells or buzzers to attract our attention. Modern telephones have electronic beepers that ring to let us know that someone is calling. In a cuckoo clock, a toy bird pops out of the clock and marks the time with the call of a cuckoo.

4 STIMULATING AND RELAXING

- For hundreds of year the steady, booming be drums gave courage to armies marching into battle.

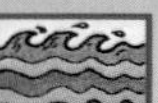

- Waves lapping again the shore, birdsong on summer's day, the crackle of a log fi on a winter's evening – these are a sounds that many people find relax

WHAT MAKES THE SOUND OF A HEARTBEAT? **SIDE ROAD** TO ROAD STOP 5

SOUND CAN STIMULATE AND RELAX THE MIND. **SIDE ROAD** TO ROAD STOP 6

Let's look at sound waves on the move...

Select
YOUR SIDE ROAD

HOW THE SOUND Travels

Imagine!
When an object making a sound travels faster than the sound itself, it produces a crashing noise called a sonic boom!

ROAD STOP 7

SIDE ROAD TO ROAD STOP 7

Can sound travel through solid objects and liquids?

Detour

SOUND TRAVELS AT DIFFERENT SPEEDS THROUGH DIFFERENT MATERIALS. LEAP TO **ROAD STOP 8**.

FOLLOW THE PATH TO THE **POINT OF INTEREST** TO FIND OUT ABOUT SOUND IN SPACE.

Sound needs a medium, such as air, to travel through. It also passes through other gases, solids, and liquids.

VIBRATIONS ON THE MOVE

Although most sounds reach our ears through the air, sound waves travel better through solid surfaces. American Indians used to put their ears to the ground to listen for distant hoofbeats.

FOLLOW THE **HIGHWAY** TO DISCOVER HOW WE HEAR SOUND.

POINT of Interest

Sound cannot travel through nothing at all.

SIDE ROAD TO ROAD STOP 8

Can sound travel through space?

No. In space, there is no air, nor any other medium, to carry sound waves. If you were able to shout your name in space, you would not hear a sound!

※ Radio waves do not need any medium through which to travel, which is why astronauts use radios to talk to each other.

※ To communicate in space without radios, astronauts would have to touch helmets together. Sound waves could then travel through the helmets and the air inside them.

SIDE ROAD TO ROAD STOP 9

WHAT IS THE SOUND BARRIER? **SIDE ROAD** TO ROAD STOP 8

HOW DOES SOUND TRAVEL? **SIDE ROAD** TO ROAD STOP 9

ROAD STOP

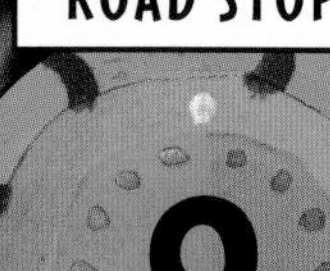

8 How fast does sound travel?

The speed of sound depends on the medium through which it travels.

LOOKING AT THE MEDIUM

The speed at which sound waves travel through a medium depends on:

1 **DENSITY** = how tightly matter in the medium is packed into a space

2 **COMPRESSIBILITY** = how easy it is to squeeze the matter into a smaller space

In general, sound travels faster through solids and liquids than through air. The molecules in solids and liquids are packed closer together and are more tightly bound than in air, so they are able to pass on sound waves more quickly.

COMPARING MEDIUMS

THIS CHART SHOWS THE SPEED OF SOUND IN VARIOUS MEDIUMS

MEDIUM	SPEED IN FEET (METERS) PER SECOND
AIR AT 59° F (15° C)	1,116 ft. (340 m)
SEAWATER AT 77° F (25° C)	5,023 ft. (1,531 m)
BRICK	11,980 ft. (3,650 m)
WOOD (MAPLE)	13,480 ft. (4,110 m)
GLASS	14,900 ft. (4,540 m)
ALUMINIUM	16,000 ft. (5,000 m)
STEEL	17,100 ft. (5,200 m)

Male humpback whales sing songs that carry for hundreds of miles through the oceans.

The speed of sound through air is 1,116 ft. (340 m) per second. It is usually measured a sea level at 59° F (15° C). Sound trave faster as the temperature increases. T speed of sound through air at 212° (100° C) is 1,268 ft. (386 m) per seco

Detour

THE SOUND THAT A MOVING OBJECT MAKES SEEMS TO CHANGE AS THE OBJECT PASSES BY. DETOUR TO **ROAD STOP 10**.

FOLLOW THE **HIGHWAY**.

DOES SOUND TRAVEL AT DIFFERENT SPEEDS THROUGH DIFFERENT MATERIALS? **SIDE ROAD TO ROAD STOP 8**

ROAD STOP

9 How does sound travel from one place to another?

Sound may pass along a wire as electrical signals, or through the air as radio waves.

1 Electrical signals

The American inventor Alexander Graham Bell (1847-1922) invented the telephone in 1876. It was the first machine to be able to carry voice vibrations as electrical signals.

HOW A TELEPHONE WORKS

- When you speak into the mouthpiece of a telephone, a microphone turns the sound waves of your voice into electrical signals.
- These pass down the telephone cable to the telephone of the person you are calling. There, a loudspeaker in the earpiece converts the signals back into sound waves that are very similar to your voice.

2 Radio waves

In 1895, the Italian inventor Guglielmo Marco (1874-1937) became the first person to send signals as waves through the air. Before then signals had been transmitted along electric w

SIDE ROAD TO ROAD STOP 9

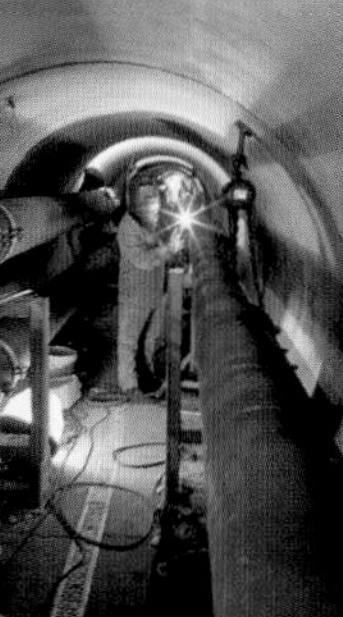

People who work underground, such as tunnel-builders, often send messages to each other by tapping on pipes. Sound travels faster and farther through metal than through air.

Visible Proof SPOT

d loses its gy less rapidly ling through a object than gh air. Ask a d to drop a n a table. You ably won't it land. Now press your ear to the . This time, you should hear the d transmitted through the table.

FOLLOW THE PATH TO THE **POINT OF INTEREST.**

POINT of Interest

Some aircraft break the sound barrier.

What is a sonic boom?

A sonic boom is a loud, thunderlike sound. It is made by an object traveling faster than the speed of sound.

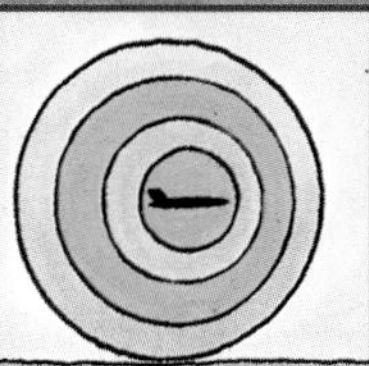

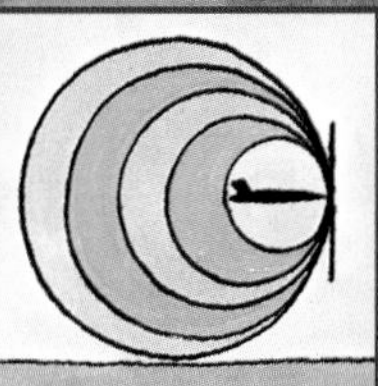

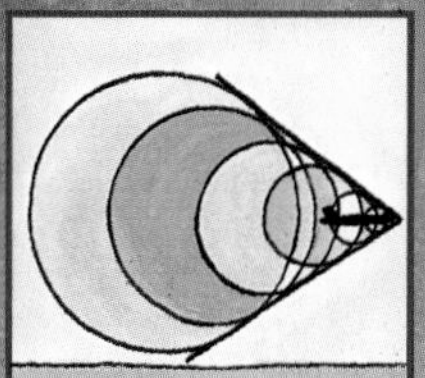

1 FLYING SLOWER THAN THE SPEED OF SOUND
Sound waves spread out ahead of the plane. The waves travel faster than the plane, so people on the ground hear the plane approaching.

2 FLYING AT THE SPEED OF SOUND
The plane moves as fast as the sound waves it produces. This causes the waves to build up in front of the plane and form a shock wave.

3 FLYING FASTER THAN THE SPEED OF SOUND
The plane leaves behind a shock wave that reaches the ground and is heard as a sonic boom. The sound does not arrive until after the plane has passed.

※ A plane exceeding the speed of sound is said to have broken the sound, or sonic, barrier. Flight faster than the speed of sound is called supersonic flight. The world's only supersonic airplane, *Concorde*, can travel at speeds of more than 1,491 miles (2,400 km) per hour.

FOLLOW THE **HIGHWAY** TO FIND OUT HOW SOUND WAVES ARE RECEIVED.

re are about two billion io sets worldwide – t's about one set for ry three people.

FIND OUT HOW SOUND CAN BOUNCE. FOLLOW THE PATH TO THE **POINT OF INTEREST.**

DOES A RADIO SET IN YOUR HOME PICK UP SOUNDS FROM A RADIO STATION DREDS OR THOUSANDS OF MILES AWAY?

crophone in the station converts the s of voices or music into electrical signals. ansmitter turns the signals into radio and broadcasts them through the air large antenna.
aller antenna on your radio set picks up ves, which the radio turns back into cal signals.
lly, a speaker in the radio transmits the cal signals as sounds.

POINT of Interest

Sound can be reflected or absorbed.

What is an echo?

An echo is a repetition of a sound caused by sound waves hitting a surface and being reflected.

Detour

REFLECTED SOUND CAN BE PUT TO IMPORTANT USES. LEAP TO **ROAD STOP 22.**

MAKING AN ECHO

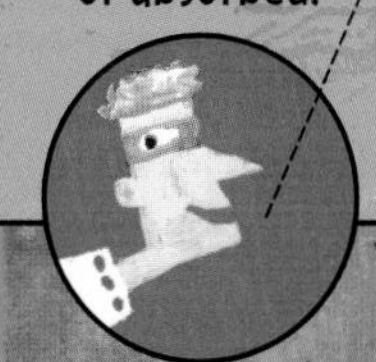

※ Smooth, hard surfaces reflect sound well. Sometimes several echoes may be heard from just one original sound. This often happens in canyons and valleys, where sound waves strike the walls at different distances and return at different times.
※ Not all surfaces reflect sound. Soft surfaces, such as fabrics and carpets, absorb sound waves so that little sound bounces back.

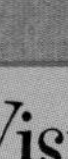

Visible Proof SPOT

This experiment shows that hard surfaces reflect sounds well and soft surfaces do not.

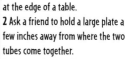

1 Arrange two long cardboard tubes at the edge of a table.
2 Ask a friend to hold a large plate a few inches away from where the two tubes come together.
3 Place a ticking clock at the end of one tube and put your ear to the other tube.
4 Sound waves from the clock travel down the first tube, bounce off the plate and travel up the second tube to your ear.
5 Now replace the plate with a cushion. This time you cannot hear the clock as loudly – the cushion soaks up most of the sound waves.

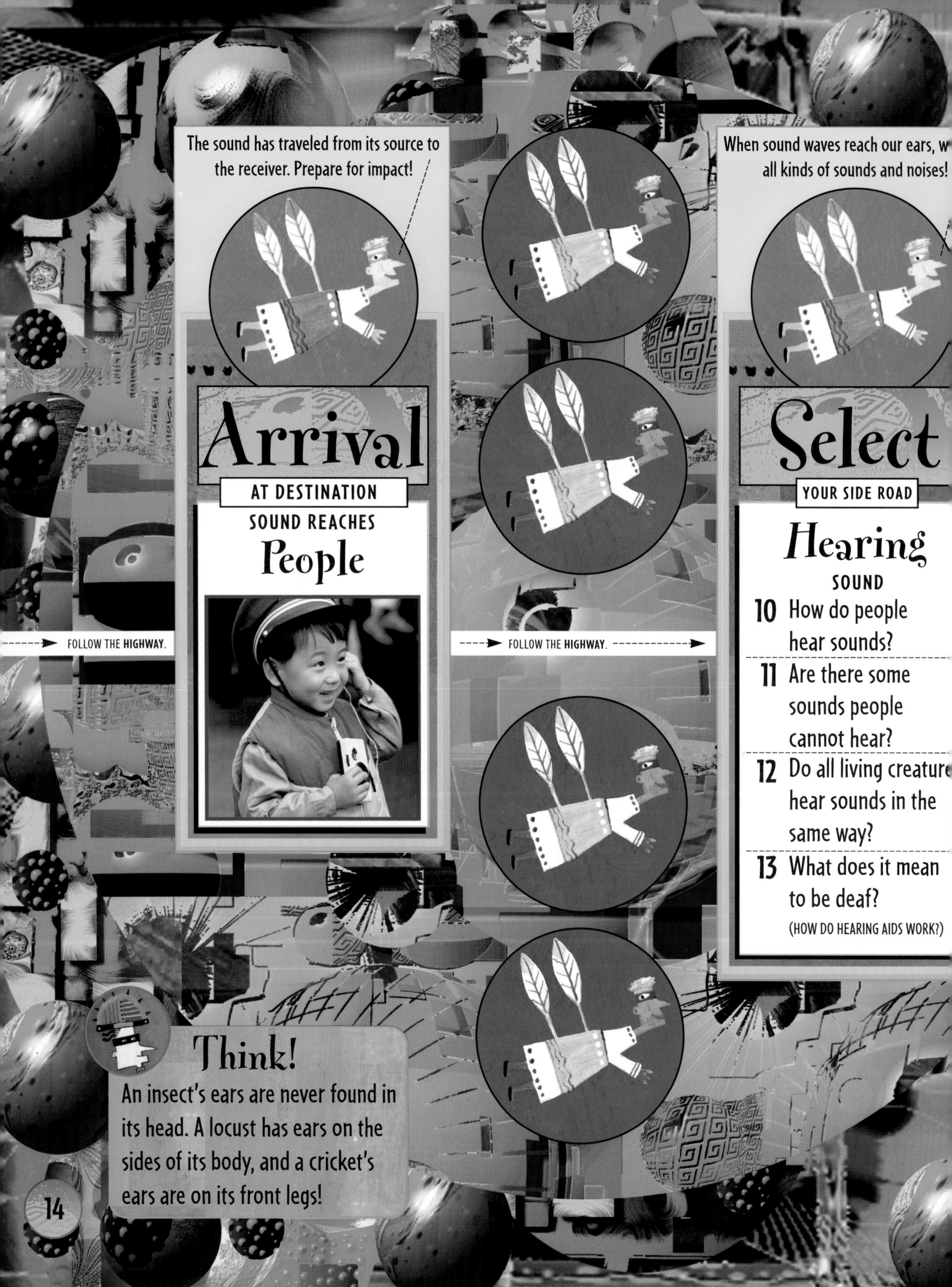

The sound has traveled from its source to the receiver. Prepare for impact!

Arrival

AT DESTINATION

SOUND REACHES

People

FOLLOW THE **HIGHWAY**.

FOLLOW THE **HIGHWAY**.

When sound waves reach our ears, w
all kinds of sounds and noises!

Select

YOUR SIDE ROAD

Hearing

SOUND

10 How do people hear sounds?

11 Are there some sounds people cannot hear?

12 Do all living creature hear sounds in the same way?

13 What does it mean to be deaf? (HOW DO HEARING AIDS WORK?)

Think!

An insect's ears are never found in its head. A locust has ears on the sides of its body, and a cricket's ears are on its front legs!

ROAD STOP

10 How do people hear sounds?

Sound waves enter the ear and are changed into nerve signals. These are sent to the brain, which interprets them as sounds.

HOW DO EARS WORK? SIDE ROAD TO ROAD STOP 10

HOW THE EAR WORKS

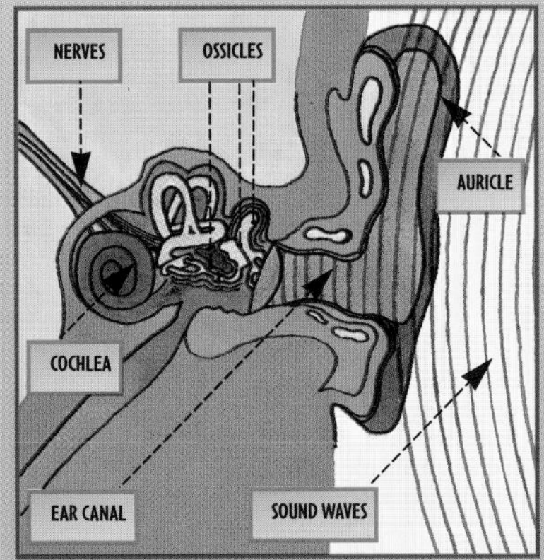

1 OUTER EAR The outer ear is made up of the visible part of the ear, called the auricle, and the ear canal.

WHAT HAPPENS The auricle acts as a funnel. It collects sound waves and directs them down the ear canal to the middle ear.

2 MIDDLE EAR The middle ear is made up of the eardrum and the ossicles, three tiny bones known as the hammer, the anvil, and the stirrup.

WHAT HAPPENS Sound waves strike the eardrum, a flap of tissue stretched tightly across the ear canal, and make it vibrate. This causes the bones in the ossicles to vibrate. The ossicles pick up and magnify the vibrations as they relay them to the inner ear.

3 INNER EAR

The inner ear is made up of the semicircular canals, which help us to balance, and a fluid-filled tube called the cochlea.

WHAT HAPPENS The vibrations create waves in the liquid in the cochlea. This movement shakes tiny hairs that line the cochlea. The hairs stimulate nerve cells, which send electrical signals, or impulses, to the brain. The brain processes the impulses into sounds.

SIDE ROAD TO ROAD STOP 10

FOLLOW THE **HIGHWAY** TO FIND OUT ABOUT SOUNDS MADE BY NATURE.

Detour

HOW DO ANIMALS HEAR SOUNDS? FIND OUT IN **ROAD STOP 12**.

HEARING SOUNDS DIFFERENTLY WHEN THEIR SOURCE IS MOVING

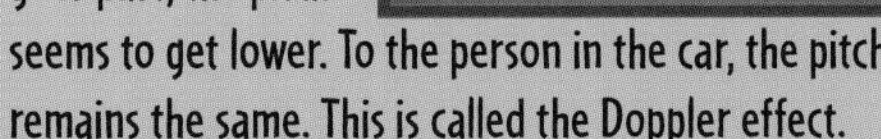

The next time a police car rushes past you, listen to the pitch of its siren. As the car approaches, the pitch seems to get higher. As the car goes past, the pitch seems to get lower. To the person in the car, the pitch remains the same. This is called the Doppler effect.

HOW THE DOPPLER EFFECT WORKS

As a police car speeds towards you, sound waves from the siren are crowded together. This increases their frequency, so you hear a higher note. When the car passes by, the waves are spaced farther apart. They have a lower frequency, so you hear a lower note.

When you hold a shell to your ear, it is not the sound of the sea that you hear, but your blood as it flows through your ears. The shell blocks out most of the other sounds around you, while the air in the shell makes the sound of the blood much louder.

Visible Proof SPOT

Create the Doppler effect by getting a friend on a bicycle to ride past you quickly, while blowing a whistle. Notice how the pitch of the whistle alters slightly as your friend passes you. What happens to the pitch if your friend cycles slowly?

SIDE ROAD TO ROAD STOP 11
SIDE ROAD TO ROAD STOP 12
WHAT SOUNDS ARE OUTSIDE OUR RANGE OF HEARING? **SIDE ROAD** TO ROAD STOP 11
CAN ANIMALS HEAR SOUNDS THAT HUMANS CANNOT? **SIDE ROAD** TO ROAD STOP 12
CAN MACHINES HELP DEAF PEOPLE TO HEAR? **SIDE ROAD** TO ROAD STOP 13

ROAD STOP 11

Are there some sounds people cannot hear?

Detour

MANY ANIMALS CAN HEAR SOUNDS THAT PEOPLE CANNOT HEAR. LEAP TO **ROAD STOP 12**.

Some sounds are too high in pitch for human ears to detect. This type of sound is called ultrasound. Other sounds are too low in pitch to be heard. This type of sound is called infrasound.

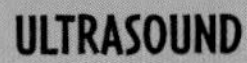

ULTRASOUND	INFRASOUND
✽ Sound with a frequency above the range of human hearing. ✽ Frequency of more than 20,000 Hz.	✽ Sound with a frequency below the range of human hearing. ✽ Frequency of less than 20 Hz.

Most people can hear sounds with frequencies between 20 20,000 Hz. This changes as people get older. A person aged 60 years can hear frequencies only up to about 12,000 Hz.

Detou

FIND OUT HOW ULTRASOUND IS USE MEDICINE. LEAP T ROAD STOP 23.

Visible Proof SPOT

To hear notes that are just inside the human range of hearing, press the very bottom and top keys of a piano The bottom key produces a low note with a frequency of about 30 Hz, wh the top key produces a high note wit a frequency of about 15,000 Hz.

FOLLOW THE **HIGHWAY** AND FIND OUT ABOUT ANIMALS AND THE SOUNDS THEY MAKE.

ROAD STOP 12

Do all living creatures hear sounds in the same way?

Different animals hear at different frequencies. Many have ears that are quite unlike human ears.

WHO HEARS WHAT?

MOST ANIMALS HEAR FREQUENCIES FAR HIGHER THAN THOSE HEARD BY PEOPLE. EXAMINE THIS CHART.

CREATURE	SOUND HEARD (HERTZ)
GRASSHOPPER	100-15,000
HUMAN BEING	20-20,000
ROBIN	250-21,000
DOG	15-50,000
CAT	60-65,000
BAT	1,000-120,000
DOLPHIN	150-150,000

MOSQUITO

Mosquitoes have sound-sensitive hairs on their antennae. Sound waves cause the hairs to vibrate. This vibration passes along the mosquito's antennae.

SNAKE

Snakes have inner ears, but no outer or middle ears. The bones of a snake's skull detect vibrations and transmit them directly to the inner ears.

WHAT ARE ULTRASOUND AND INFRASOUND? **SIDE ROAD** TO ROAD STOP 11
DO MOSQUITOES HAVE EARS? **SIDE ROAD** TO ROAD STOP 12
SIDE ROAD TO ROAD STOP 13 TO LEARN ABOUT DEAFNESS

ROAD STOP

13

What does it mean to be deaf?

Some people are totally deaf, which means they cannot hear any sounds. Other people are partly deaf, or hard of hearing, which means they can hear some sounds.

Detour

LOUD SOUNDS CAN DAMAGE THE EAR. DETOUR TO **ROAD STOP 18.**

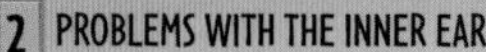

WHAT CAUSES DEAFNESS?

1 PROBLEMS WITH THE OUTER OR MIDDLE EAR

* The ear canal can become blocked with ear wax. Doctors remove the wax by washing the ear out with jets of water.
* If the middle ear becomes infected, it may fill with fluid. This stops the ossicles from transmitting vibrations to the inner ear.

2 PROBLEMS WITH THE INNER EAR

* A damaged cochlea may not be able to convert sound vibrations into nerve impulses, so the brain has nothing to interpret.
* Deafness may also occur if the auditory nerve, which carries impulses from the cochlea to the brain, is damaged.

LIVING WITH DEAFNESS

FOLLOW THE PATH TO THE **POINT OF INTEREST.**

* Speech therapists teach deaf people to lip-read.
* Many deaf people communicate using a combination of sign language and finger spelling.

* SIGN LANGUAGE uses gestures and hand signals to represent objects and ideas.
* FINGER SPELLING uses hand signals to represent different letters of the alphabet.

Visible Proof SPOT

Try to lip-read a whispered message from a friend.
Your friend should face you and mouth slowly and clearly.

FOLLOW THE **HIGHWAY.**

POINT of Interest

Machines can improve hearing.

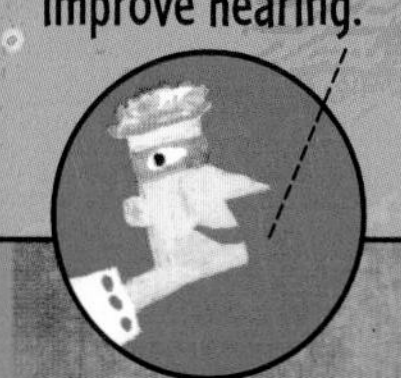

How do hearing aids work?

Hearing aids are devices that make sounds louder for people who are hard of hearing.

Detour

WHAT MACHINES DO WE USE TO AMPLIFY MUSIC? DETOUR TO **ROAD STOP 25.**

THE HISTORY

* Hearing aids were first used in the 1600's. People used horn-shaped devices called ear trumpets.
* The first electronic hearing aids, called vacuum-tube aids, appeared about 1920. They were large and difficult to carry.
* Transistor hearing aids appeared in the 1950's and were small and cheap. They have completely replaced vacuum-tube aids.

HOW A HEARING AID WORKS

1 The earpiece of the hearing aid fits in the ear canal. The rest of the aid slips behind the ear. A small battery powers the hearing aid.

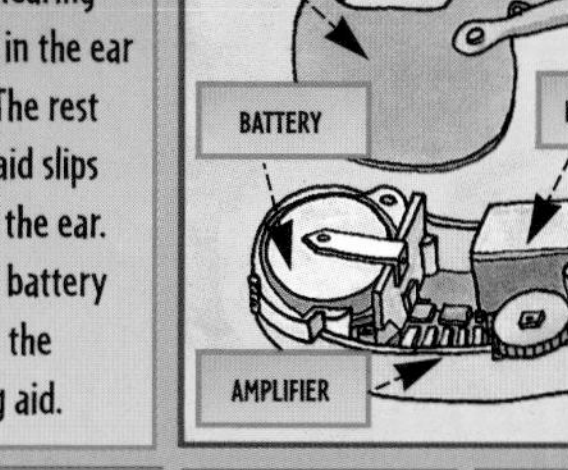

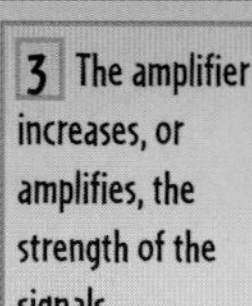

2 The microphone converts sounds into electrical signals.

3 The amplifier increases, or amplifies, the strength of the signals.

4 The receiver turns the signals back into sounds, which should now be loud enough for the person to hear.

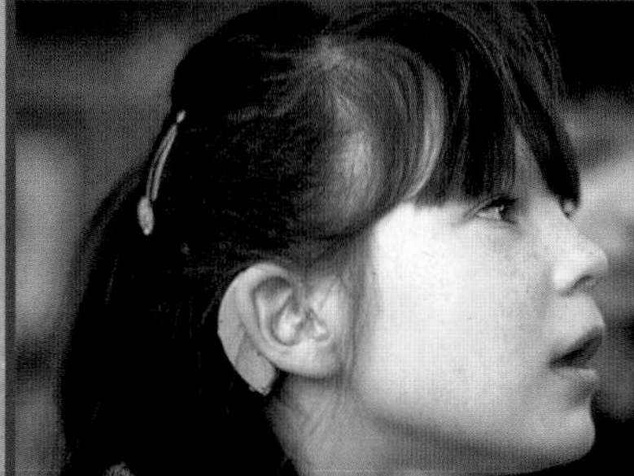

* Very loud sounds can permanently damage your hearing. Never put your ear close to a loud noise.

Visible Proof SPOT

An ear trumpet amplifies sound by gathering sound waves from a large area and channeling them into the ear. Make an ear trumpet by rolling a C-shaped piece of paper into a cone. Place the narrow end of the trumpet to your ear and point the wide end at a sound.

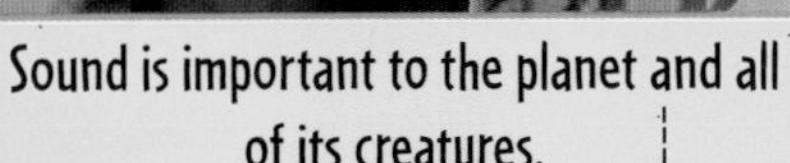

Sound is important to the planet and all of its creatures.

Select

YOUR SIDE ROAD

Sounds

ON PLANET EARTH

14 Do different parts of the world have different sounds?
(ARE SOME SOUNDS RECOGNIZABLE EVERYWHERE?)

15 Why do sounds appear and disappear through time?

16 How do animals use sound?

SIDE ROAD TO ROAD STOP 14

SIDE ROAD TO ROAD STOP 15

SIDE ROAD TO ROAD STOP 16

Imagine!

No one knows what dinosaurs really sounded like – we can only imagine their roars and screeches!

ROAD STOP

14

Do different par of the world hav different sounds

SOME SOUNDS ARE THE SAME WHEREVER YOU HEAR THEM. FOLLOW THE PATH TO THE **POINT OF INTEREST.**

The sounds you hear depend on where you are and the activities that are going on around you.

FOLLOW THE **HIGHWAY** TO DISCOVER THE EFFECT THAT SOUND CAN HAVE ON PEOPLE.

POINT of Interest

That sounds familiar!

Are some soun recognizable everywhere?

You can identify some sounds no matter where you are in the world.

Detour

ANIMALS USE SOUNDS IN MANY WAYS, FOR MANY REASONS. LEAP TO **ROAD STOP 16.**

A DOG BARKING

Dogs make a range of sounds, including barks, yelps, growls, howls, and whines. The sounds may mean different things in different situations – a whine may mean that a dog is in pain, wants something, or that it wishes to play.

A SIREN WAILING

Most police cars, fire engines, an ambulances use high-pitched sire to alert traffic. Lighthouses and s use low-pitched sirens, called fog to warn other ships about bad we or obstacles.

In the rain forest

NDS YOU MAY HEAR...

The piercing screams of macaws.

The roars of leopards.

The hiss of snakes.

The beating of hummingbird wings.

The croak of tree frogs.

The rustling of leaves.

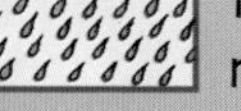
The patter of raindrops.

In the city

SOUNDS YOU MAY HEAR...

The thud of footsteps.

The roar of traffic.

The honking of car horns.

The blare of music from radios.

Voices talking or shouting.

The clatter of machinery.

The banging of doors.

Visible Proof SPOT

Take a walk around your neighborhood and make a note of the different sounds you hear. Repeat the walk at various times throughout the day. Do the sounds that you hear in each case change depending on the time of day it is?

NATURE'S SOUNDS

VOLCANOES
Powerful forces within the Earth create volcanoes. In 1883, Krakatau, in Indonesia, erupted with such force that the explosion was heard almost 3,000 miles (4,800 kilometers) away.

WAVES
The movement of air over seas and oceans creates waves. They may lap gently as they break over each other. The wind may whip up the water into large waves that rise and smash against each other, lashing harbor walls and grinding pebbles together on the seashore.

FOLLOW THE **HIGHWAY**.

LISTENING TO THE WEATHER

UNDER
air is heated by a flash of lightning, nds rapidly and creates giant sound in the air. We hear these sound waves ap, crackle, or rumble of thunder.

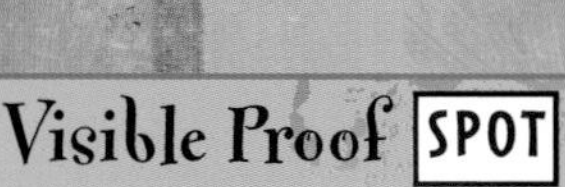

Visible Proof SPOT

up a paper bag and pop it nching it. Like thunder, ursting bag makes a loud d as it sends sound waves ing through the air. The d is created by the air cules in the bag being rapidly squashed together hen released when the bag rips open.

2 WIND
A tornado is a powerful, twisting windstorm. Howling winds swirl in the shape of a funnel, reaching speeds of over 200 miles (320 kilometers) per hour.

Detour

HOW CAN SOUND CAUSE AN AVALANCHE? FIND OUT IN **ROAD STOP 18**.

ARE SOME SOUNDS NO LONGER HEARD? **SIDE ROAD** TO ROAD STOP 15

WHY IS SOUND SO IMPORTANT TO ANIMALS? **SIDE ROAD** TO ROAD STOP 16

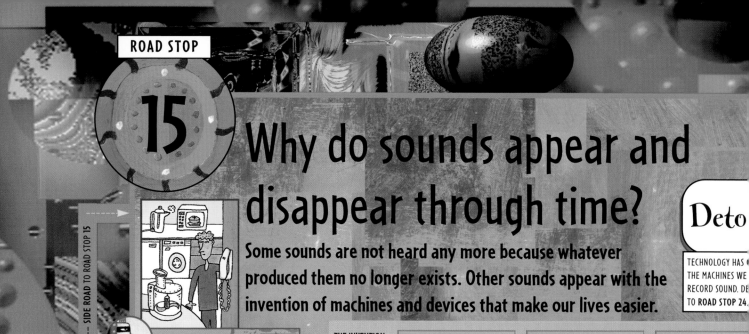

ROAD STOP

15 Why do sounds appear and disappear through time?

Some sounds are not heard any more because whatever produced them no longer exists. Other sounds appear with the invention of machines and devices that make our lives easier.

SIDE ROAD TO ROAD STOP 15

Visible Proof SPOT

Listen to the sounds made by objects in different rooms in your home. Which sounds would you not have heard 10 years ago? You may need to ask an older brother or sister, or your parents.

THE INVENTION OF DIFFERENT FORMS OF TRANSPORTATION OVER THE CENTURIES CREATED MANY NEW SOUNDS.

1 SLITHERING AND SLIDING
DATE: BEFORE 5000 B.C.
During prehistoric times, people used sledges to drag loads along the ground. They were usually made from logs or animal skins.

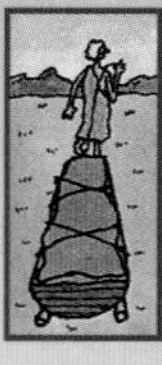

2 CREAKING OF WHEELS
DATE: ABOUT 3500 B.C.
The people of Mesopotamia, in the Middle East, built the first wheeled vehicles. These early carts were pulled by oxen.

3 THUDDING OF HOOV
DATE: 1100's
European wagon-makers built the first horse-drawn carriages. The iron horseshoe, invented in about 900, he to protect horses' hooves.

Deto

TECHNOLOGY HAS THE MACHINES WE RECORD SOUND. DE TO **ROAD STOP 24.**

FOLLOW THE **HIGHWAY** TO FIND OUT ABOUT THE EFFECTS OF SOUND ON PEOPLE'S LIVES.

ROAD STOP

16 How do animals use sound?

Animals use sounds to tell each other who and where they are, and how they are feeling. Sound can warn of danger, signal a challenge, or mark out territory. Many animals use sound to attract a mate.

HOW DOES A CRICKET USE ITS WINGS TO SING? SIDE ROAD TO ROAD STOP 16

SIDE ROAD TO ROAD STOP 15

1 Danger, danger!

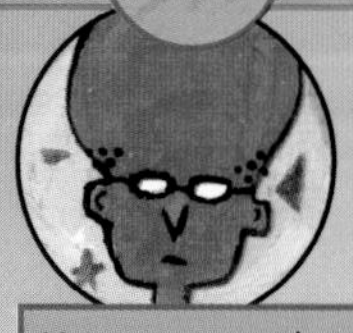

African vervet monkeys have three main predators – eagles, leopards, and snakes. To warn each other about the kind of danger they face, the monkeys use three distinct alarm calls.

PREDATOR: Eagle.
CALL: Chuckling sound.
ACTION: Dive for cover in bushes.

PREDATOR: Leopard.
CALL: Loud bark.
ACTION: Clamber up nearby trees.

PREDATOR: Snake.
CALL: High-pitched chatter.
ACTION: Stop and search the ground.

2 Look at me!

Male frogs use their voices mainly to attract mates. Each species has its own call, from croaks, grunts, and clicks to squeaks, whistles, and trills. The males of many species have vocal sacs in their chins or cheeks. The frogs blow air into the sacs, which inflate like balloons and amplify the sound of their voices.

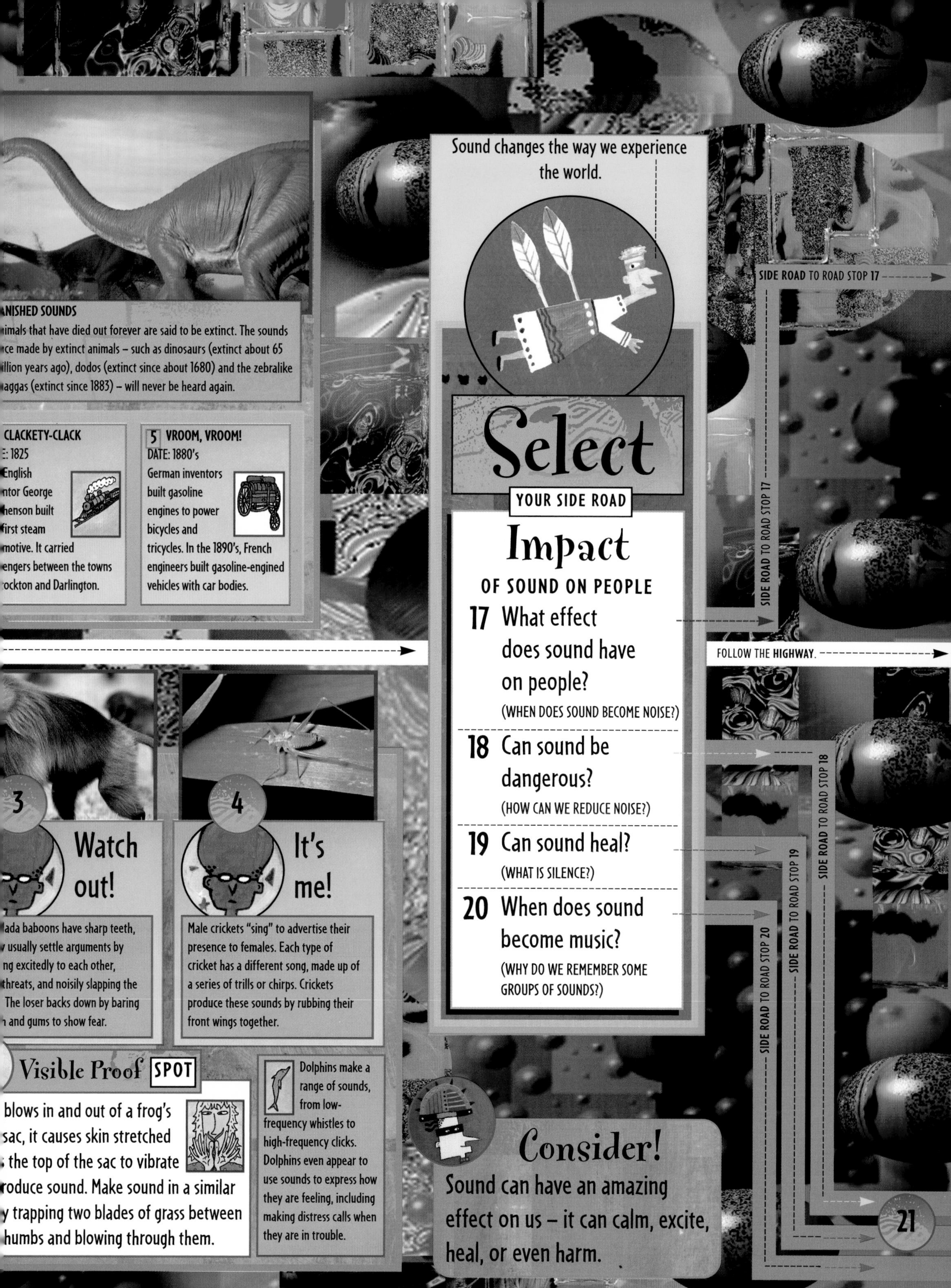

NISHED SOUNDS

imals that have died out forever are said to be extinct. The sounds ce made by extinct animals – such as dinosaurs (extinct about 65 illion years ago), dodos (extinct since about 1680) and the zebralike aggas (extinct since 1883) – will never be heard again.

CLACKETY-CLACK

E: 1825

English ntor George henson built first steam motive. It carried engers between the towns ockton and Darlington.

5 VROOM, VROOM!

DATE: 1880's

German inventors built gasoline engines to power bicycles and tricycles. In the 1890's, French engineers built gasoline-engined vehicles with car bodies.

3 Watch out!

ada baboons have sharp teeth, y usually settle arguments by ng excitedly to each other, threats, and noisily slapping the The loser backs down by baring h and gums to show fear.

4 It's me!

Male crickets "sing" to advertise their presence to females. Each type of cricket has a different song, made up of a series of trills or chirps. Crickets produce these sounds by rubbing their front wings together.

Visible Proof SPOT

blows in and out of a frog's sac, it causes skin stretched the top of the sac to vibrate roduce sound. Make sound in a similar y trapping two blades of grass between humbs and blowing through them.

Dolphins make a range of sounds, from low-frequency whistles to high-frequency clicks. Dolphins even appear to use sounds to express how they are feeling, including making distress calls when they are in trouble.

Sound changes the way we experience the world.

Select

YOUR SIDE ROAD

Impact

OF SOUND ON PEOPLE

SIDE ROAD TO ROAD STOP 17

SIDE ROAD TO ROAD STOP 18

SIDE ROAD TO ROAD STOP 19

SIDE ROAD TO ROAD STOP 20

FOLLOW THE **HIGHWAY**.

Consider!

Sound can have an amazing effect on us – it can calm, excite, heal, or even harm.

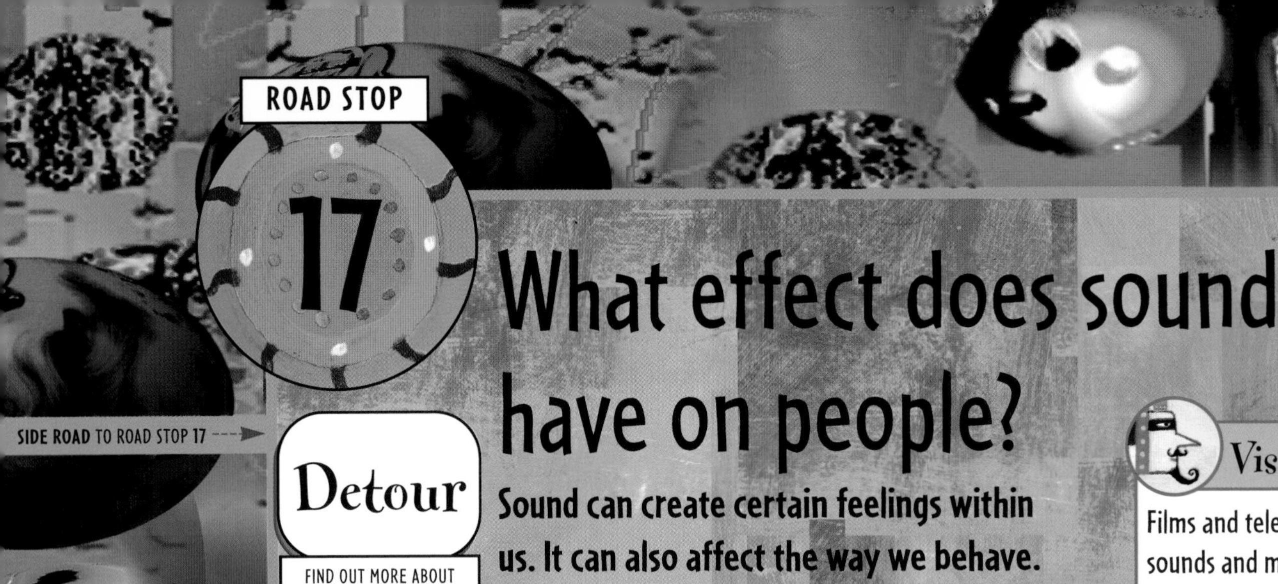

ROAD STOP

17

What effect does sound have on people?

Sound can create certain feelings within us. It can also affect the way we behave.

SIDE ROAD TO ROAD STOP 17

Detour

FIND OUT MORE ABOUT MUSIC IN **ROAD STOP 20**.

Detou

CAN SOUND HEAL? LE
ROAD STOP 19.

SOUND CAN BECOME A NUISANCE. FOLLOW THE P
TO THE **POINT OF INTERE**

Many people respond to lively, rhythmic drumbeats by automatically tapping their feet, clapping their hands, or dancing. In Africa, music and dance play an important part in festivals that celebrate events such as births and harvests.

Some sounds make people wince and feel uncomfortable, such as metal scraping on metal, or fingernails on a blackboard.

A loud, sudden sound, such as a bang, may make a person yell out and even jump into the air.

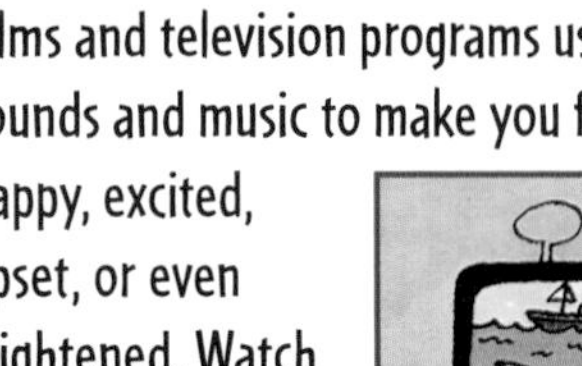

Visible Proof SPOT

Films and television programs use sounds and music to make you feel happy, excited, upset, or even frightened. Watch a film or T.V. show with your eyes closed. Can you tell what is happening just by listening to the music?

FOLLOW THE **HIGHWAY** TO DISCOVER HOW PEOPLE COPY, AMPLIFY, AND USE SOUND.

ROAD STOP

18

Can sound be dangerous?

A sound of 140 decibels or more crosses the threshold of pain. This means that it produces pain in the ear. Constant noise, even if it is not loud, can cause headaches, sickness, and hearing loss.

Detou

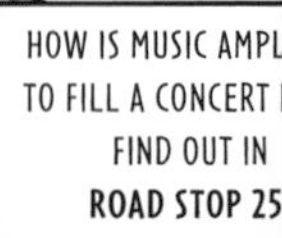

HOW IS MUSIC AMPL
TO FILL A CONCERT
FIND OUT IN
ROAD STOP 25

HOW DO PEOPLE
REDUCE NOISE? F
THE PATH TO THE
OF INTEREST.

WHEN DOES SOUND BECOME DANGEROUS? **SIDE ROAD** TO ROAD STOP 18

An avalanche is a sudden, huge fall of snow and ice down the side of a mountain. Most avalanches happen in warmer weather, when snow melts and becomes unstable. A disturbance, such as a loud noise, can send the snow sliding.

DANGEROUS SOUND

※ A rock band can play music up to 120 dB in volume. Rock musicians and people in the audience can suffer from temporary, or even permanent, deafness.

※ Playing a personal stereo too loudly over a long period of time can damage the hearing. Sound levels inside the ears are more intense because earphones send sound directly into the ears.

SIDE ROAD TO ROAD STOP 19
SIDE ROAD TO ROAD STOP 20

POINT of Interest

Sound that is annoying!

When does sound become noise?

Noise is any sound that is random or unwanted.

RANDOM SOUND

A pleasing sound, such as a musical note, is made up of regular, gently curving sound waves.

A random sound, or noise, such as that made by a machine, has irregular, spiky sound waves.

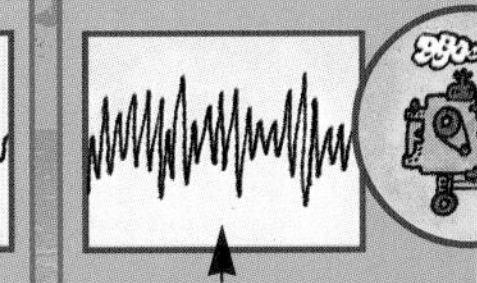

UNWANTED SOUND

Unwanted sound can be anything, from musical notes to the hammering of a drill. A sound is unwanted, or becomes noise, if a person listening to it finds it distracting, annoying, unpleasant, or loud.

ELECTRICAL NOISE

Electrical noise is unwanted sound that is produced by radiation and disturbances in the air. These are caused by many things, including lightning, the sun, telephones, and computers. Electrical noise interferes with the reception of transmitted signals.

LUNAR LISTENING

Astronomers use radio telescopes on Earth to tune in to signals from space. The telescopes have to separate the signals from electrical noise in the atmosphere. In the future, astronomers may build observatories on the far side of the moon, which is shielded from Earth's noise.

Visible Proof SPOT

Tune in to different radio stations. The hissing sound you hear on some stations is electrical noise interfering with the radio signals.

FOLLOW THE **HIGHWAY**.

POINT of Interest

Protect yourself from pain!

How can we reduce noise?

Noise pollution is noise that is unpleasant to people near it. It may come from machinery, cars, planes, or even other people. Noise pollution can be controlled in a number of ways.

Detour

FIND OUT MORE ABOUT SILENCE. SIDE ROAD TO **ROAD STOP 19**.

1 MAKING LAWS

Many countries have laws that forbid people to make noises above certain decibels during the evening. Some laws set the upper sound levels for vehicles such as trucks. Other laws set sound levels in factories to protect the health of the workers.

2 PROTECT YOURSELF

People who are surrounded by loud noises protect their ears by wearing ear protectors, such as ear plugs or ear muffs. Ear muffs have a thick layer of padding to absorb sound.

3 PEACE AND QUIET

Buildings can be insulated from outside noise by having thick walls, well-sealed doors, and double-glazed windows.

A DOUBLE-GLAZED WINDOW IS MADE OF TWO PANES OF GLASS.

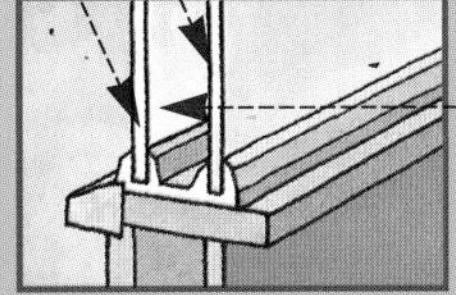

SOUND DOES NOT TRAVEL AS EASILY THROUGH THE AIR BETWEEN THE PANES AS IT DOES THROUGH GLASS.

FIGHTING NOISE WITH ANTI-NOISE

Two noises can be added together to create silence! A microphone measures the sound wave of a noise, then a computer creates a mirror image of the wave and plays it back. The two sounds overlap and cancel each other out. This method is called anti-noise.

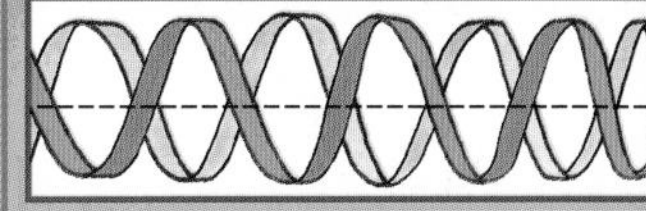

THE PEAKS (HIGHS) IN THE ORIGINAL SOUND WAVE CORRESPOND TO TROUGHS (LOWS) IN THE GENERATED WAVE.

IS THERE REALLY SUCH A THING AS SILENCE? **SIDE ROAD** TO ROAD STOP **19**

WHEN DOES A GROUP OF SOUNDS BECOME MUSIC? **SIDE ROAD** TO ROAD STOP **20**

ROAD STOP

19

Can sound heal?

Sound can relax us and make us calm. Some people believe that sounds have properties that make us feel better and more healthy.

A CALMING EFFECT

Mothers often soothe crying babies by talking or singing to them in hushed tones. Babies respond particularly well to low notes and repeated sounds.

MUSIC THERAPY

Some hospitals use music to stimulate patients. Patients may let out pent-up emotions by shouting, laughing, crying, or dancing in response to music. Others sing or play musical instruments to help develop better control of their breathing and muscles.

ANCIENT SOUNDS

The Chinese use sound as part of Chi Kung, the ancient art of self-healing. Chi Kung teaches that sounds can strengthen and heal vital organs in the body. Each organ has its own healing sound and position. Chi Kung is also used to relax the mind and body.

Visible Proof SPOT

Make the sounds of Chi Kung to relax yourself. Stand in the positions show and repeat each sound three times, using long, drawn-out breaths.

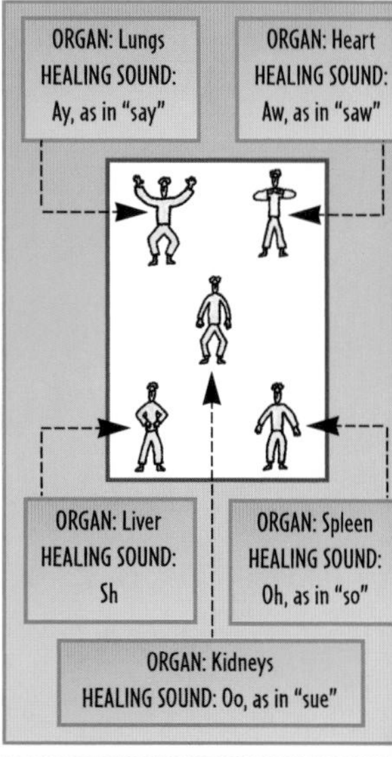

DO SOME PEOPLE LIVE IN SILENCE? FOLLOW THE PATH TO THE **POINT OF INTEREST**.

FOLLOW THE **HIGHWAY** TO DISCOVER HOW PEOPLE ORGANIZE SOUND INTO SPEECH.

ROAD STOP

20

When does sound become music?

Music is sound arranged into interesting or pleasing patterns. Musical sounds, or notes, may be produced by human voices, musical instruments, machines, and even nature.

Detour

WHAT TYPE OF INSTRUMENT IS A SYNTHESIZER? LEAP TO **ROAD STOP 26**.

COMPOSING

A composer selects certain sounds and combines them to create a piece of music. How the music sounds depends on:

- the composer's skill and talent
- the musical instruments available
- the musical traditions of the country
- the function of the piece of music

MAKING MUSIC

When an instrument is played, part of it is set vibrating. Every instrument produces a different pattern of vibrations and sound waves. These patterns can be recorded as wave patterns on an oscilloscope.

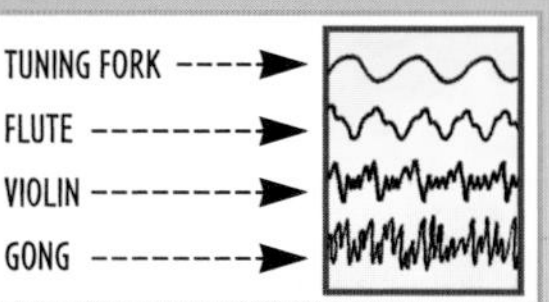

1 WIND INSTRUMENTS

Sound is made by blowing into a hollow object, making the air inside vibrate.

A flute player blows air across a hole. To make notes of different pitches, the player presses keys that cover holes in the instrument. This changes the length of the column of vibrating air inside the flute.

2 STRING INSTRUMENTS

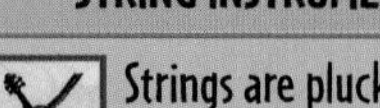

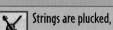

Strings are plucked, bowed, strummed, or struck, causing them to vibrate.

A violin player produces notes by drawing a bow, made from horsehair, across the string. The bow makes the strings vibrate and give out sounds, which are then amplified by the hollow body of the violin.

SIDE ROAD TO ROAD STOP 19

HOW DO MUSICAL INSTRUMENTS MAKE SOUNDS? **SIDE ROAD** TO ROAD STOP 20

POINT

Interest

When sound disappears.

What is silence?

Silence is the absence of any sound.

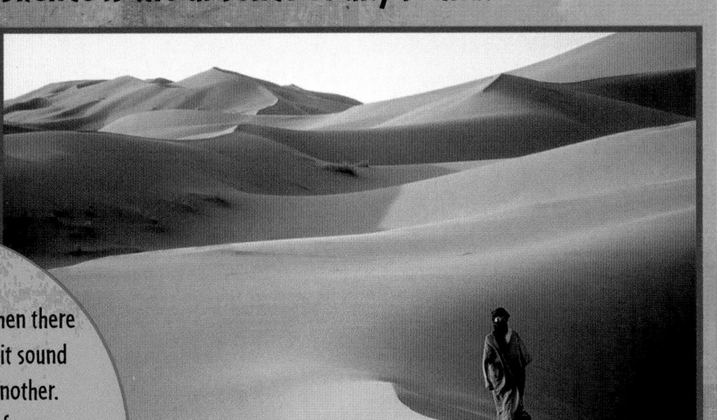

TOTAL SILENCE

True silence exists only when there re no molecules to transmit sound waves from one place to another.

※ If all the air is removed from a tainer, it becomes a vacuum. Sound ves cannot travel through a vacuum.

※ Human beings cannot experience silence because we cannot exist in a vacuum.

There is never total silence on Earth. There is always some sound to be heard. Deserts are among the quietest places on Earth. But even they have sounds of insects that live there and grains of sand sliding over each other.

Detour

CAN YOU COMPOSE MUSIC FROM SILENCE? LEAP TO **ROAD STOP 27**.

LIVING IN SILENCE

Monks and nuns are people who devote their whole lives to religion. Many monks and nuns observe a rule of silence, which means that they spend a large part of their time in silent prayer.

PYRAMID POWER

※ The King's Chamber in the Great Pyramid at Giza, Egypt, is extremely well sound-proofed. If you stood perfectly still inside the chamber, you would hear just the sound of your own breathing. Soon you would also hear a loud rushing noise, like a waterfall. It would be the sound of the blood flowing through your body, echoed many times by the walls of the chamber!

FOLLOW THE **HIGHWAY**.

FOLLOW THE PATH TO THE **POINT OF INTEREST**.

Visible Proof SPOT

e your own wind instrument. everal glass bottles with different unts of water. Blow gently across ops of the bottles. The air inside bottle vibrates and makes a rent musical note. The more air there is in a bottle, lower it vibrates and the lower the note.

KEYBOARD INSTRUMENTS

Keyboard instruments have a series of keys ected mechanically to a ce that produces sound.

sing the keys of a piano keyboard ates levers that move small, padded, den hammers. These strike metal strings e piano, which vibrate to produce notes.

4

PERCUSSION INSTRUMENTS

Percussion instruments include anything that can be shaken, hit, clicked, or scraped.

Striking timpani, or kettledrums, with mallets produces a deep, echoing sound. A player can change the pitch by pressing a pedal, which tightens or relaxes the skin of the drum.

POINT

of Interest

Keeping musical memories.

Why do we remember some groups of sounds?

A random collection of sounds is difficult to remember because it is unpredictable. Music is easier to remember because it is usually made up of patterns of sounds.

REMEMBERING TUNES

※ We remember some songs and tunes because they mean something to us. They can re-create memories and emotions.

※ Songs often have catchy choruses. These are known as "hooks," because they are easy to hum and remember.

Detour

HOW DO WE CONTROL LIVE SOUND? DETOUR TO **ROAD STOP 25**.

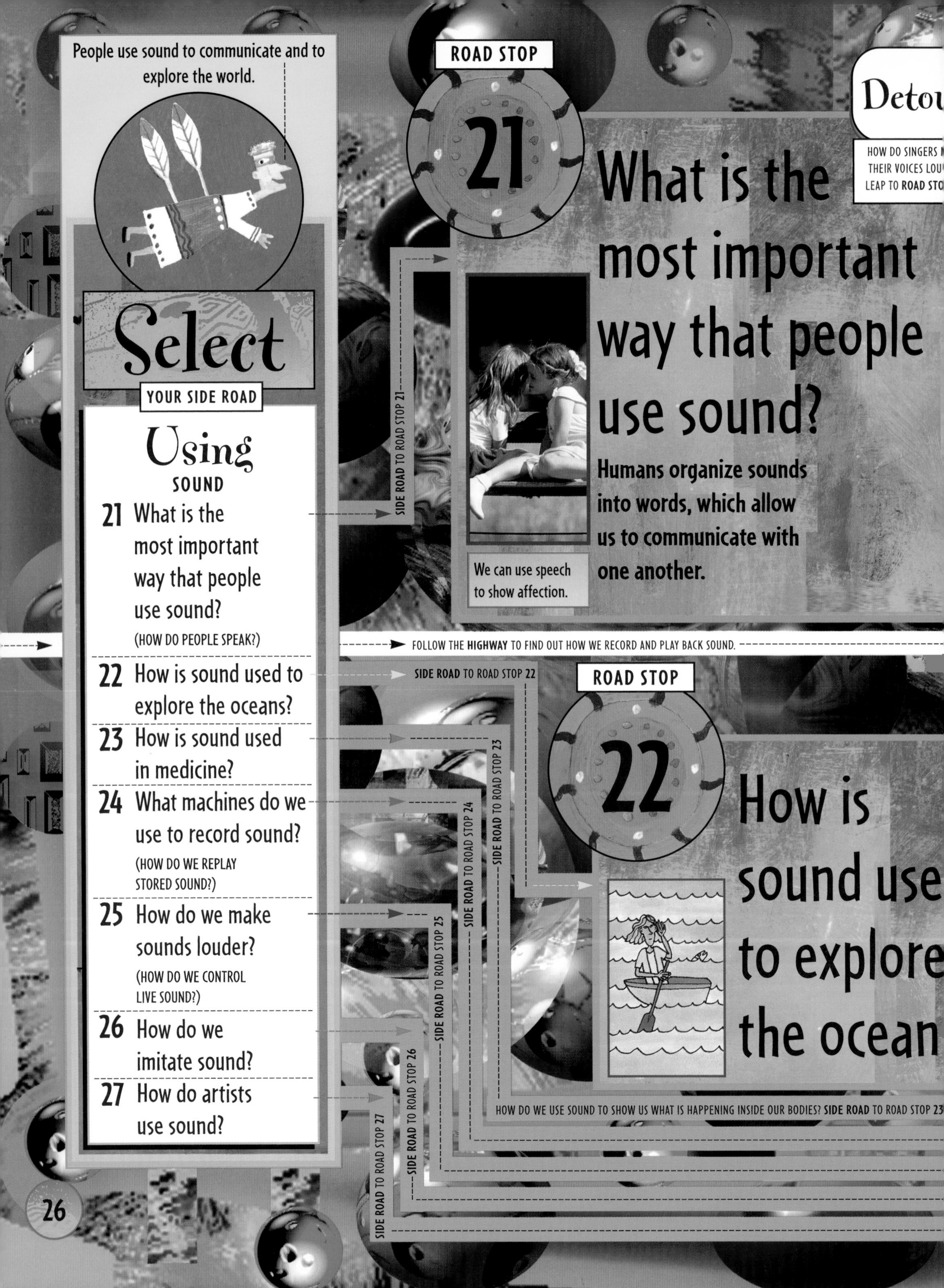

People use sound to communicate and to explore the world.

Select
YOUR SIDE ROAD

Using SOUND

SIDE ROAD TO ROAD STOP 21

ROAD STOP 21

What is the most important way that people use sound?

Humans organize sounds into words, which allow us to communicate with one another.

We can use speech to show affection.

Detou

HOW DO SINGERS THEIR VOICES LOU LEAP TO **ROAD STO**

FOLLOW THE **HIGHWAY** TO FIND OUT HOW WE RECORD AND PLAY BACK SOUND.

SIDE ROAD TO ROAD STOP 22

ROAD STOP 22

How is sound use to explore the ocean

HOW DO WE USE SOUND TO SHOW US WHAT IS HAPPENING INSIDE OUR BODIES? **SIDE ROAD** TO ROAD STOP 23

SIDE ROAD TO ROAD STOP 23

SIDE ROAD TO ROAD STOP 24

SIDE ROAD TO ROAD STOP 25

SIDE ROAD TO ROAD STOP 26

SIDE ROAD TO ROAD STOP 27

LANGUAGE

Humans are the only animals to use sound to create a spoken language, ...ch. The word "language" from the Latin word *lingua*, ...g tongue. All languages have ... things in common.

...PATTERN = the sounds that the speech organs can make. Most ...ges have between 20 and 60 of ...ounds.

... = sound-patterns that have a ... meaning. Words may represent ..., actions, or ideas.

...AR = the rules by which words ... their forms and are combined ...ntences. Each language has its ...ammar.

TO FIND OUT HOW WE USE OUR MOUTHS TO SPEAK, FOLLOW THE PATH TO THE **POINT OF INTEREST**.

We can use speech to show aggression.

POINT of Interest

It's good to talk to each other!

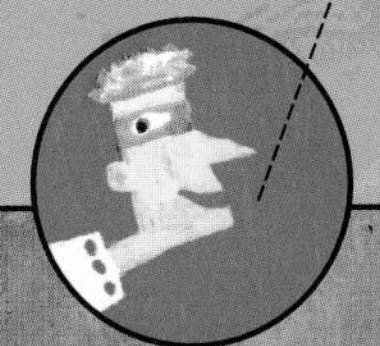

How do people speak?

The sound of the voice is produced mainly by the vibration of the vocal cords. The mouth, tongue, teeth, and lips shape the sound into words.

1 When you breathe in, muscles in the larynx (L) relax the vocal cords – small folds of tissue that stretch across the larynx (X).

2 When you speak, the muscles tighten the vocal cords (X). As air passes over the cords, it makes them vibrate and produce sound.

Visible Proof SPOT

Stretch the neck of a blown-up balloon between your fingers. As the air escapes, it makes the neck vibrate and produce a shrieking sound. Change its pitch by tightening or relaxing your grip. The neck of the balloon acts like the vocal cords, and your fingers act like the larynx muscles.

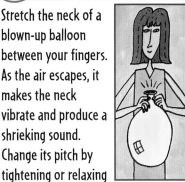

ROAD STOP

23 How is sound used in medicine?

...hins use a ...nique called ...location ...cate fish ...nderwater ...acles. ...tists use a ...ar principle ...xplore ...oceans.

WHAT IS ECHOLOCATION?

※ A dolphin produces short bursts of ultrasound that bounce off objects and create echoes. The dolphin listens to the echoes to figure out the size, distance, and direction of the objects.

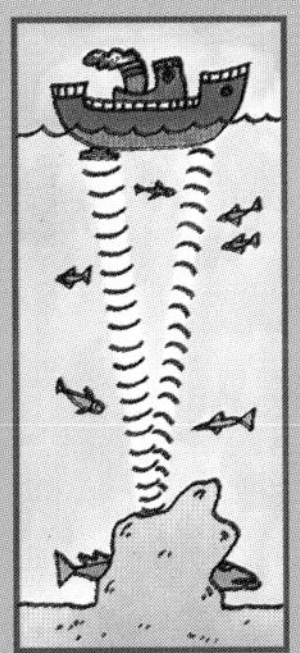

※ A ship's sonar device sends waves of ultrasound into the water. The time taken for the sound waves to be reflected back from the ocean bed, or from obstacles in their path, indicates the depth of the ocean bed or the distance from the obstacles.

SIDE ROAD TO ROAD STOP 23

Doctors use ultrasound to examine the inside of a patient's body.

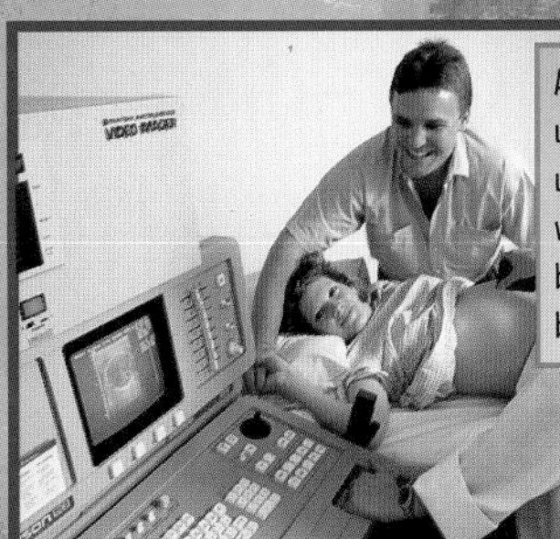

A scanner is able to show an image of an unborn baby inside its mother. It transmits ultrasound waves into the mother's womb, where they are reflected by the baby's body. The scanner interprets the echoes to build up a picture of the baby on a screen.

Ultrasound can also help to detect cancer, heart disease, and other conditions.

HOW DO WE STORE SOUND? **SIDE ROAD** TO ROAD STOP 24
HOW DOES AN AMPLIFIER WORK? **SIDE ROAD** TO ROAD STOP 25
HOW DO WE USE MACHINES TO REPLICATE SOUNDS? **SIDE ROAD** TO ROAD STOP 26
SOUND CAN CREATE WORKS OF ART AND MOVE PEOPLE. **SIDE ROAD** TO ROAD STOP 27

ROAD STOP

24

What machines do we use to record sound?

Detour

FIND OUT HOW SOUNDS CAN BE MADE ELECTRONICALLY. LEAP TO **ROAD STOP 26**.

For centuries, people could only listen to music live – as it was being played. From the 1870's, it became possible to record music. Today, sound can be stored in many ways and then played back at any time.

1

MECHANICAL RECORDING

In 1877, the American inventor Thomas Edison (1847-1931), pictured above, invented the first practical sound-recording machine, the phonograph. Sound made into a mouthpiece caused a needle to vibrate. This etched a groove in a foil-covered rotating cylinder. The phonograph developed into the record player, which stores sounds as jagged waves in a spiral groove on a plastic disc.

2

MAGNETIC RECORDING

In magnetic recording, sound is stored on audio tape, a thin plastic ribbon coated with metallic particles that can be magnetized. A tape recorder receives sound as electrical signals. These signals change the strength of the magnetic field around the recording head. As the tape travels past the head, the field magnetizes the particles on the tape into a pattern like that of the sound waves.

3

DIGITAL RECORDING

Digital recording machines turn sound into a numerical, or digital, code. Each number in the code gives the height of a sound wave at a given point. Digital code may be stored on compact disc (CD), digital audio tape (DAT), or digital compact cassette (DCC).

Digital code i
recorded on
surface of a C
millions of ti
which are lai
in a spiral tra

FOLLOW THE F
THE **POINT OF**

FOLLOW THE **HIGHWAY** TO FIND OUT HOW MACHINES COPY SOUNDS.

WHAT DID THOMAS EDISON INVENT? **SIDE ROAD** TO ROAD STOP 24
WHAT IS AN AMPLIFIER? **SIDE ROAD** TO ROAD STOP 25

ROAD STOP

25

How do we make sounds louder

Singers and musicians use machines called amplifiers to make their voices and music louder. Record, cassette, and compact disc players contain small amplifiers that strengthen electrical signals.

A microphone converts the sound waves of the singer's voice into weak electrical signals.

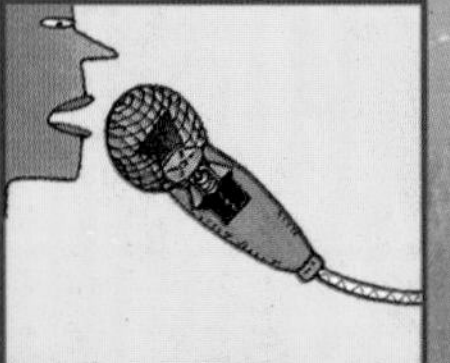

An amplifier uses electronic components called transistors to make stronger copies of the signals.

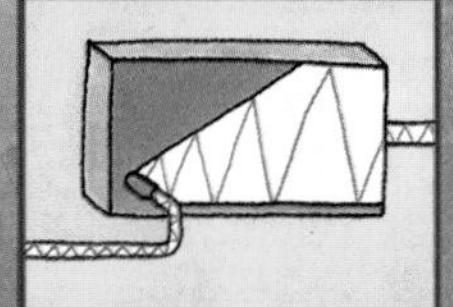

The transistors feed the strengthened signals to the speaker.

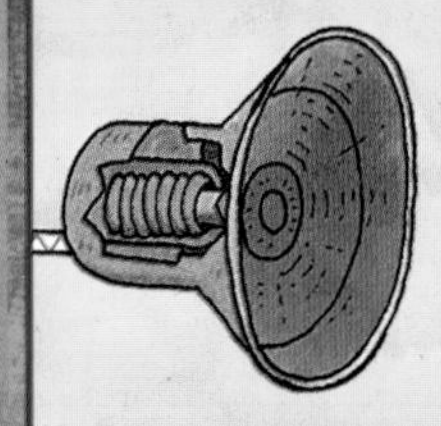

The speaker turns the signals back into sound waves, which are now much louder.

BOOSTING SIGNALS

A tape recorder uses an amp
to boost the weak electrical
signals from the microphone
before they can be recorded
During playback, weak signa
again strengthened by an
amplifier to make them stro
enough to drive the speaker

SOME SOUNDS CAN BE RECREATED IN SIMPLE WAYS. **SIDE ROAD** TO ROAD STOP **26**
HOW DO MOVIE THEATERS USE SOUND? **SIDE ROAD** TO ROAD STOP **27**

POINT of Interest

It's playback time!

How do we replay stored sound?

Sound stored on record, tape, or disc is played back through speakers – devices that turn electrical signals back into sound.

STEREOPHONIC SOUND

Music is usually recorded by using at least two microphones, spaced apart. The recordings are then combined and played back through at least two speakers, also spaced apart. This produces stereophonic sound, a lifelike sound that has depth and direction.

LISTENING TO A RECORD

As a record spins on the record player, a needle, called a stylus, rides along the groove. The stylus follows the waves in the groove and vibrates. These vibrations are turned into electrical signals that speakers convert back into sound.

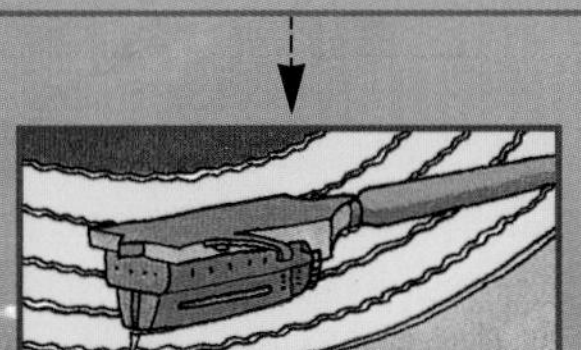

LISTENING TO A TAPE

When a tape is played back in a tape recorder, it passes the playback head. The magnetic patterns on the tape produce electrical signals in the head. The signals are relayed to speakers, where they are broadcast as sound.

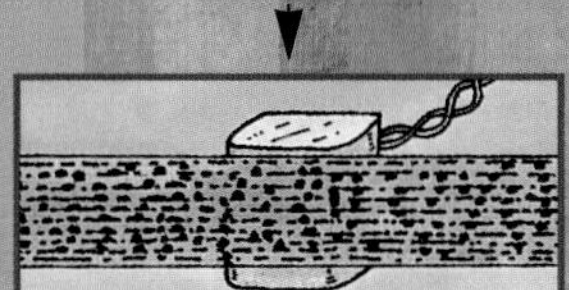

LISTENING TO A DISC

A laser beam scans the surface of a CD as it spins at high speed. The pits on the disc scatter the beam, while the flat areas reflect it. A detector turns these flashes of light into electrical signals that speakers turn back into sound.

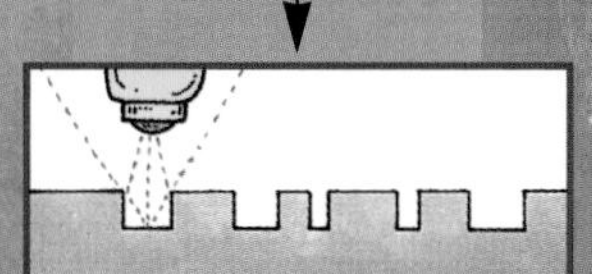

Visible Proof SPOT

Two ears give us stereophonic hearing, which means we can tell where a sound is coming from. Shut your eyes and ask a friend to clap in different places around you. You should be able to locate the sound just by listening. How easy is it if you cover up one ear?

FOLLOW THE PATH TO THE **POINT OF INTEREST.**

Visible Proof SPOT

aphone is
ice that
fies the
. It focuses
l waves
rd and
them from
ding out too
. Make a megaphone by rolling
aped piece of paper into a cone
ecuring it with tape. Speak into
arrow end of the cone.

POINT of Interest

It's all a question of control.

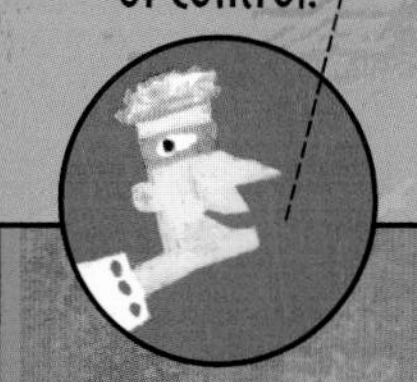

How do we control live sound?

Amplifiers can control only the volume of sound. The quality of sound that is heard depends a lot on the room or building in which it is played. This is known as architectural acoustics.

The acoustics of a room are affected by:
- its size and shape
- the materials on its walls and ceiling
- its ability to keep out unwanted sound
- its ability to control reflected sound

REFLECTION AND ABSORPTION

A concert hall or theater is designed to provide good architectural acoustics. Panels, disks, or balls hanging from the ceiling reflect the sound waves towards the audience. Some sound waves are absorbed by the chairs, curtains, carpets, and even people's clothes.

SIDE ROAD TO ROAD STOP 26
SIDE ROAD TO ROAD STOP 27

ROAD STOP

26

How do we imitate sound?

Some machines and devices can copy sounds and then use them in new and exciting ways.

SYNTHESIZERS

A synthesizer is an electronic instrument, usually played by means of a keyboard. A synthesizer can reproduce the sounds of traditional instruments, such as a flute or guitar. It can also create completely new sounds. Electronic components inside the synthesizer generate electrical signals that produce the sounds.

Many pop and rock artists and groups use synthesizers in their music.

SAMPLING

A sampler is a device that can digitally record any sound, from birdsong to breaking glass. The sound is then played back using a keyboard. A synthesizer can change the digital code of a sampled sound to produce sounds of different pitch and quality.

SOUND EFFECTS

Sound-effects specialists are people who cr
sounds for radio and television programs. T
computers, synthesizers and samplers to cr
most of their sound effects. They may also
everyday objects to make convincing sound
such as thunder or galloping horses.

FOLLOW THE **HIGHWAY** TO THE END OF YOUR JOURNEY.

ROAD STOP

27

How do artists use sound?

Musicians, performers, and visual artists use sound to convey messages, feelings, and experiences.

CONDUCTING SILENCE

In 1952, the American composer John Cage (1912-1992) wrote a work called *4′ 33.″* It requires the performer to sit silently at a piano for 4 minutes and 33 seconds, without playing a note. The audience is invited to listen to sounds in the hall, such as the lid being raised or people coughing, and also to noises from outside.

SOUND AS ART

In her work *Mutual Interest* (1997), the Israeli artist Michal Rovner shows footage of birds in flight accompanied by the sound of beating wings. The film is projected in a small room, with the sound played at full volume. It echoes off the walls and sounds like whirring helicopter blades or gunfire.

SOUND AND MOVING IMAGES

SILENT FILMS

The first films were shown publicly in the mid-1890's. Early filmmakers could not match sound to the pictures, so theaters employed pianists or orchestras to accompany the images on screen.

THE "TALKIES"

The first successful film to use recorded sound was *The Jazz Singer* (1927), starring Al Jolson. Sound that had been mechanically recorded on a disc was played along in time with the film strip.

SOUND-ON-FILM

By 1929, most films u
system called sound
Electronic signals re
the sound directly o
film strip.

SIDE ROAD TO ROAD STOP 26

SIDE ROAD TO ROAD STOP 27

an make realistic sound effects simple materials.

DER = flap a large sheet ck cardboard.

ALL = pour dried peas onto a d metal tray.

OPING HORSES = clap two s of a coconut shell her; for a jingling harness, a bunch of keys.

ING ON SNOW = squeeze wist a roll of cotton batting.

HING ARMY = rhythmically a box of small stones.

ING OBJECT = crumple candy pers and snap dried twigs.

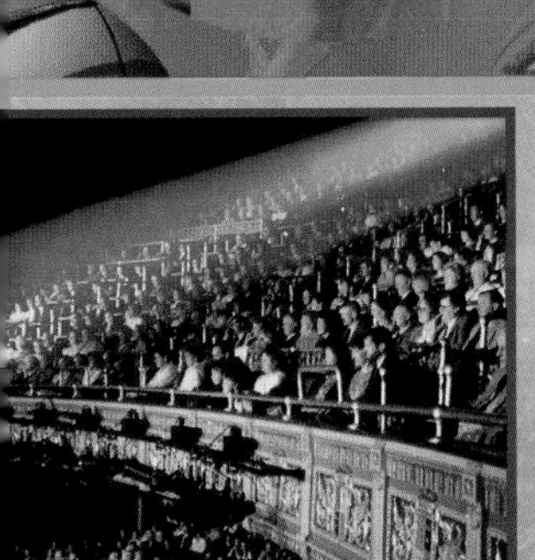

L SOUND
ovie theaters use a complicated ent of many speakers to produce realistic, three-dimensional sound, round-sound. The sound itself is recorded long the edge of the film strip.

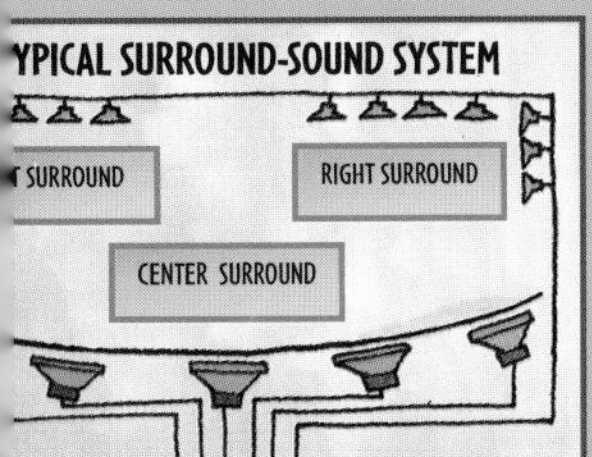

From the point at which **sound** is made to the Impact Zone – you!

The rumble of traffic, the buzz of a bee, the blast of a trumpet... a journey that can elevate, educate, irritate, entertain, and move us.

Think!

As sound technology advances, and as further uses for ultrasound and infrasound are developed, sound will have an increasing effect on our planet. It will create a richer environment for us to live in.

Index

PICTURE CREDITS Front Cover: left and center: Science Photo Library; right: Images Colour Library. Back cover: Tony Stone. Inside: p3 top: Tony Stone; bottom: Science Photo Library. p5: Rex Features. p6 bottom left and right: Pictor International. p7 top: Pictor International; bottom: Tony Stone. p8: Science Photo Library. p9: Images Colour Library. p10 left and right: Tony Stone. p11: Images Colour Library. p12: Planet Earth Pictures. p13 top left: The Stock Market; top right: Tony Stone; bottom left: Betty Images/Panos Pictures. p14: Tony Stone. p15 top: Science Photo Library; center: The Stock Market. p16 top and bottom left: Tony Stone; bottom right: Images Colour Library. p17 top: Trip; bottom: Sally & Richard Greenhill. p18: Tony Stone. p19 top and bottom: Tony Stone. p20 left: Planet Earth Pictures; right: Tony Stone. p21 top left: Oxford Scientific Films; bottom left: Planet Earth Pictures; right: Tony Stone. p22 top: Tony Stone; bottom left: Science Photo Library; bottom center: Rex Features; bottom right: Pictor International. p23: Pictor International. p24: Pictor International. p25 top left and right: Tony Stone. p26: Pictor International. p27 left and right: Tony Stone. p28 top left: Science Photo Library; top right: Tony Stone. p29 top right: Hulton Getty; top left: Rex Features; bottom left, bottom center and bottom right: Kobal Collection. p30: Pictor International.